Ha Ha: the book of humor

Eric Marton Cunningham
Comedy Stage name Sir Eric The Cunningham

Waldenhouse Publishers, Inc.
Walden, Tennessee

Ha Ha: the book of humor
Copyright © 2018 by Eric Marton Cunningham. All rights reserved. No part of this book may be reproduced in any form or by any electronic or mechanical means including information storage and retrieval systems, without permission in writing from the publisher. The only exception is by a reviewer, who may quote short excerpts in a review.
Published by Waldenhouse Publishers, Inc.
100 Clegg Street, Signal Mountain, Tennessee 37377 USA
888-222-8228   www,waldenhouse.com
ISBN: 978-1-947589-22-3
Library of Congress Control Number: 2019951368
  Humorous freedom of speech containing over 50 topics of jokes, small paragraphs and funny stories in African American vernacular --Provided by publisher
Printed in the United States of America
HUM000000 HUMOR / General
FIC060000 FICTION / Humorous / Black Humor
HUM004000 HUMOR / Form / Jokes & Riddles

Dedication

To

YOU AND EVERYONE THAT READS THIS BOOK

Contents

Introduction 7
Preface 9
1. Every Day Life 11
2. Spiritual Humor 23
   A. Hero for any problem Bruce Leroy 26
   B. Joe and Josephine 28
3. Short stories 31
4. Things people deal with in life 44
5. About the weather 64
6. Things about animals 85
7. Professional Jobs 123
8. Sports 183

introduction

You can Ha Ha at work, Ha Ha on break, Ha Ha on the bus, Ha Ha on an Airplane, Ha Ha in the Park, Ha Ha in School, Ha Ha in College, Ha Ha in the Doctor's office, Ha Ha at the Football Game, Ha Ha at the Basketball Game, Ha Ha at the Hockey Game.

Sir Eric
the Cunningham-comedy stage name

Preface

Ha Ha is a book of Humorous freedom of speech

Freedom – Quality or state of being free; liberty; independence; ease of movement; a right.

Speech – Act or way of speaking; power to speak in public; to talk.

This book is for the purpose is LAUGHTER to make you HAPPY when you're sad, to read to someone when they're sad.

This Book can help increase your reading skills. If you have a problem reading or know someone who does, this book can take away that problem.

If anything in this Book you find offensive to you, I am sorry. It is only for Humor; please except My APOLOGY. Please enjoy the Book Ha Ha.

GOD BLESS YOU TODAY AND EVERYDAY,
THAT'S MY MOTTO.

1.

Every Day Life

If I was the King of the streets	12
Time	13
Bad kids	15
Men working	17
Women shopping	19
Women cooking	21

If I Was King Of The Streets

If I was the King of the streets, there would be no more illegal drugs, and everyone could get a free Big Mac so everyone would come back.

If I was the King of the streets, there would be no more people killed by the police, so everyone could live in peace and party every day.

If I was the King of the streets, on Friday in the streets there would be a fish fry party and everyone could get full and party hardy to the break of dawn.

If I was the King of the streets, the schools would have Bruce Leroy so when the kids are bad, he could give them some Act Right.

If I was the King of the street, church could be open every day, so people not working can take time out and go pray every day.

If I was the King of the streets, no guns would be around so there would be happiness and love all over the World so people could keep on having fun.

If I was the King of the streets, a good man would always get a freebie (SEX THAT IS).

If I was the King of the street ... so VOTE FOR ME.

Time

Time is power. Can time put power in me? YES, just look at the clock and see how you feel.

Time is seconds. Can time make me run fast? YES, only if you have fast feet.

Time is hours. Can time let me sleep late if I want to? YES, if you can still keep your Job.

Time is always on time. Can time help me be on time if I'm late? Yes, just don't get caught turning the clock back.

Time is numbers. Does time see the future? Yes, it's time for you to find something to do; you're wasting time.

Time has been here forever. What will happen if we run out of time? Change the battery in your clock.

All over the world time is different. How will we know what time it is in other places? Just go there and see.

Tick, tock, tick, tock, that's the sound of a clock makes. Is there any other sound? YES, buy a Rolex and listen; it goes around and don't stop. Rolex goes around silent that the sound they make.

Can time help me to get to work since, I'm always late? Yes, just get up early so you can leave home early.

Can time help me to get to over my girlfriend's house on time? Yes, just move in with her.

Can time help me to pay my bills on time? Yes, get a job?.

Can time help me cut the grass on time? YES, get a lawnmower that works.

Can time help me to feed my kids right? YES, take cooking classes.

Can time help me to budget my money better? YES, stop going to the mall every day.

Can time help me to save gas in going to work? YES, get a good job in the City.

Can time make me a star? YES, move to Hollywood on Sunset Boulevard.

Bad Kids

What are bad kids?

Kids that will not do what they're told, steal things that don't belong to them and curse out the parents. That's bad.

These kids were so bad they would take a dog and make it act like a cat.

These kids were so bad, at dinner time McDonald's would close up because sometime their mother did not cook.

These kids were so bad the neighbors who lived next to them would leave their home when these kids came home from school.

These kids were so bad their mail came by airplane drop off, because they would always take the mail truck.

These kids were so bad that the school gave them start A's so they would not have to come to school at all.

These kids were so bad that they made up their own games called I can be badder then you.

These kids were so bad they did not have Father's Day or Mother's Day; they had Kids Can Be Bad Every Day.

These kids were so bad they never had to go to the store. The store came to them because it saved on store repairs; the kids always broke things.

These kids were so bad they would go to school and tell the teacher what to do.

These kids were so bad that the police had to call for back up just to get a little kitten out of the tree, and the kitten was trying to get away from the kids.

These kids were so bad they were stealing cars at the age of five years old.

These kids were so bad that their parents had to get permission from the kids to stay up.

These kids were so bad that the people next door were always out because the kids next door ate them out of house and home.

These kids were so bad the crime rate was so low in the neighborhood because no one ever told on those kids.

These kids were so bad that they all had college degree's because the college would give it to them so they would stay away from their college.

These kids were so bad that Wal-Mart changed the name to KIDS MART so they would have their own store to shop in.

Men Working

Men's working – Is that hard to do? NO, they just have to get a Job.

Men working – does that have to do with physical labor? NO, some have set down jobs.

A man working – is that a life time thing? NO, some men never work at all.

Men working – where can you find that activity? Anywhere you see men not standing still or sitting down or when they are getting a butt call.

Men working – do they get paid for working? YES, only if they're not lock up and working for free.

Men's working – is that outside or inside? If it is raining inside, if they can see lady's outside.

Men working – do women do this? YES, if their husband let them.

A man working – can you do this day and night? YES, day time its labor night times it's a butt call.

Men working goes on when you want to build something or tear something down. Do they do it just to get paid? Yes if they are working.

Men working happen day or night. Day time they clock in and then take a break; at night time they take a break before they clock in.

Men working will always be going on; the only time it will stop is when they have to work for free.

Men working – women complain about men always working. Sometimes they're not working they are out getting a freebie (sex) or a butt call.

Men working – can kids be part of men's working? Only if they are of age and if they will not quit when they get their first pay check.

Men working – will there be a time where they get overtime? You can always get over time as long as you come to work on time.

Men's working today is very different because women are doing what men are doing, so men don't want women to know if they are not at work; they are getting a butt call.

Men working – I believe that hard labor is now easy labor because the man makes the machine to do the work only if the man has a degree from the old school.

Women Shopping

What is women shopping?

It is when women get paid and they spend up all their money at the mall in one day and show it off and the next day take it all back.

Is shopping all that women do? NO, shopping is 90% of it; the other 10% is getting more money from her husband or boyfriend.

Do women ever shop for anyone else? YES, for children school supply's, so when they go to school they can go shopping again.

How can a women know when there is a sale? They pay people to tell them in advance.

Is it wrong for women that shop too much? YES, no money, no credit card, no sale, no life.

Are sales only for women? Only if they get there first.

What make women shop so much? So their husbands or boyfriend can watch sports or go get a butt call.

Can a woman ever shop without it being a sale? YES, only if it's their first time.

A woman shopping – is there a day that women don't shop? YES, when there is nothing for them to buy.

Women shopping – do women spend a lot of money shopping? YES, their's and their husband or boyfriend.

Women shopping – do they spend a lot of time shopping? YES, Some time all day just looking for something to buy.

Women shopping – do women go to a lot of places to shop? YES, anywhere there is a sale.

Women shopping – do women get along shopping? YES, until two women see the same thing they want, at the same time and they both want it. Then they got a big fight on their hands.

Women shopping – do women take children when they're shopping? YES, only if they're less than 1 year old. That's when they can't ask for anything.

A woman shopping – is there any time they go shopping with their husband or boyfriend? YES, if he agrees to carry all the bags and sit in one place quietly.

A woman shopping – is there a time women are not shopping? YES, when they're asleep although 90% of time they dream they're shopping.

Women Cooking

Women cooking – women that can't even boil water think they can cook.

Women cooking – if your nephews ask can we go over to Joey's house next door when its dinner time, is that a sign that Aunt can't cook?

A woman cooking – when your boyfriend comes over for dinner and always brings fast food is that a sign you can't cook.

A woman cooking – whenever you have a party everyone brings food when the party's over everyone's food is gone but yours. Is that a sign you need cooking classes?

Women cooking – it's Thanksgiving; everyone is at your house; it's time to eat. You go in the kitchen to get the food. You come out and everyone has gone next door to eat. Is that a sign that you can't cook?

Women cooking – if your husband brings home his boss for dinner, the next day your husband comes home from work and says he got fired. Is that a sign that you can't cook?

A woman cooking is a great art of food preparation. What happens when cooking is your problem? None, just buy fast food, or get in a cooking class.

They say the way to a man heart is through his stomach. If you keep losing boyfriends does that means you can't cook? That's a good question.

Cooking is a part of life and if you cook for someone and they love you they will eat it, although if they eat it and they think that it's going to kill them, you need a cooking class.

When you cook for someone and they have to go to the rest room a lot, you need a cooking classes ASAP.

Is it ok for a wife to cook for your husband boss? Only when he leaves and your husband still has job.

Cooking is so much fun only if when you get through it and you eat it and that is great. Although if your guest have to go to the hospital, you need a cooking class now.

Women cooking can be good for someone although it may not for someone else. Cooking for your boyfriend is ok, and it is great when he get a butt call too.

Women cooking sometimes have to be tested, because if you thank you can cook and never have cooked before, that meal could be dangerous to someone's health.

2.

Spiritual Humor

God blessings   24
The Hero of any problem
   A. Bruce Leroy   26
   B. Joe & Josephine   28

God Blessings

Will God bless you with a soul mate? YES, but you have to work out the Love part.

Will God bless you with a good job? YES, but you have to do the work.

Will God bless you with a car? YES, but you have to put the gas in it.

Will God bless you with a good home? YES, but you have to keep it clean.

Will God bless you with children? YES, but you have to make them act right.

Will God bless you when you get in trouble? YES, but you have to stay out of trouble.

Will God bless with the winning power ball numbers? NO, God don't gamble.

Will God bless you to be a handsome or beautiful person? YES, but you have to get your own hair cut and your own hair weaves.

Will God bless you to be a super Athlete? YES, but how much you work out is on you.

Will God bless you to see the future? YES, just learn from the past.

Will God bless you to stay out of jail? YES, just don't break the law.

Will God bless you to be the President of the United States? YES, just don't listen to politics.

Will God bless you to be a Millionaire? YES, just start saving money now.

If I prayed to God will I be blessed with a new car? YES, but you have to pay the car note.

Will God bless you with a very good paying job? YES, although getting paid is up to you.

After all of this praying for a beautiful or handsome person in my life, when is God going to bless me with the person? God has. They too passed by you every day; you just did not say HELLO.

If I pray to be a movie star will God bless me? YES, just find an agent in Hollywood. Tell them God sent you and they will hook you up.

Will my life be rich and famous if I pray to God? YES, because He's never late and always on time.

Are all blessing from God? YES, unless you have been praying to the Devil.

Can God help me with my kids? They are always being bad. No, call Bruce Leroy; he will come over and give them some Act Right.

God is the power of the world. If I pray to him will he stop all this violence? YES, although he can help stop what is in your house; the rest call 911.

Is God, Jesus, and the Holy Spirit are they all the Powers of God? YES, although you can only talk to them one at a time; just get on the main line.

The Earth is a part of the Galaxy that God created. Are there any more places that God has made? YES you can see all that in your ETERNAL life; stay prayed up.

God is good all the time; all the time God is good. If you do the same, all your blessing will come before you ask.

Bruce Leroy

Who is Bruce Leroy?

He is the world's best Martial Art Hero that you can call any time for help and save you from your problem.

If you can't find a knife to cut your watermelon open, call Bruce Leroy. He can open it with a Karate chop.

If you lose your keys and can't get in your house, call Bruce Leroy; he can open it with a Bruce Leroy Kick.

If your kids are so bad and will not act right, call Bruce Leroy he can give them some ACT RIGHT HI YAAA!

If you have someone that is always bothering you, Call Bruce Leroy; give him the name and address – no more problem.

If you always have a party and the same person always come and mess up the party, call Bruce Leroy. Your party will be fine. If that person shows up, Bruce Leroy will give him some Get Out HA YAAA!

If you have a problem of your house getting broken into when you go out of town, call Bruce Leroy. He can give them that break into your house something called Stay Out!

If you have a problem finding a baby sitter, call Bruce Leroy. Your kids will have a good time, and when you get back, and your kids are being bad, tell them you're going to call Bruce Leroy, and they will act right.

When you go out to buy a new car and the car salesman gives you a hard time, just call Bruce Leroy. He will give them a good deal of Act Right and you will get the best car on the lot.

When you go out to the movies premier and the people around you are so loud you can't even hear the movie, just call Bruce Leroy. He will give them some Shut Up – problem solved.

When it's a week day in a work week and your neighbors are arguing late at night; it's 1:00 am; it been going on for hours, and you called the police, and they still going at, just call Bruce Leroy. He will come over and he make them to make love, not war – problem solve.

You have a dog, and your neighbor have a dog, but you neighbor dog always beat up your dog, call Bruce Leroy. He will train your dog to win – problem solved. The Act Right never fails.

If your son plays on a football team and they're always losing and your son comes home says Mama and Dad our team needs some help; we always losing. Just call Bruce Leroy. He will give the coach something to help your team win some DOUBLE ACT RIGHT – problem solved.

When you go fishing and your friend always out fish you every time, and you've tried everything, call Bruce Leroy. He will get you the book with the title *How to Catch One* – problem solved.

There is a beautiful girl you have fallen in love with but she just keep playing hard to get. You have spent almost a thousand dollars on her. You tried everything, Call Bruce Leroy; he will give her some Act Right to at least be your friend or pay your money back or act right. Ether way you haven't lost – problem solved.

Joe & Josephine

Joe and Josephine went up the hill. This time they wanted to play. Joe said Josephine let me get a butt call and we can make a boy today.

Joe and Josephine went down the hill and made love again. This time Josephine was on the top and made Joe do some work. This time they had twins.

Joe and Josephine went to the mall to buy the kids some clothes and the girls wanted red. While Josephine was shopping, she saw Joe looking at other women and smacked him up side his head.

Joe and Josephine had a party eating and drinking and having fun. Everyone was having a ball. When the party was over Josephine gave Joe a butt call.

Joe and Josephine they took a trip and came to Nashville. They stayed out all day then all night. Let's do it again; that was to them a thrill. So it was Friday night and they was out in the streets. Josephine said lets go back to the room. She give Joe a butt call; they had a boy his name is Bill.

Joe and Josephine had so many kids and they started acting bad. She tried everything; she talked to one of her girlfriend she had met in Tennessee. She said if you are having problems with your kids call Bruce Leroy. He said having problems with bad kids? He came over and look at the kids and said this is going too rough. He gave them some Double Act Right for five minutes – problem solved.

Joe and Josephine they got a puppy. The kids loved him a lot; they take him everywhere they go. They left him at home; he tore up the house. They said we can't do this no moe.

Joe and Josephine went to the movie. The title was *The King of Martial Arts Bruce Lee Story*. Josephine said that wasn't the Man we called for our kids was it? Joe said NO we call Bruce Leroy. Bruce Lee trained Bruce Leroy – problem solved.

Joe and Josephine went to school to see their kids in a play Christmas. All of their kids was great in the play; they still talk about it every day.

If Joe wasn't Joe and Josephine wasn't Josephine who would they be? We've got a problem; let's call Bruce Leroy. They told him the problem. Bruce Leroy said it would be Josephine and Joe problem to solve . He said they really need some act right.

Josephine and Joe was at home, the kids gone to sleep; they have the house to their self. Joe want to watch the football game. Josephine wanted to watch the Opera. They could not make up their minds. They tried everything and it did not work so they said, let's call Bruce Leroy. They told him the problem. He brought over another big screen TV so they could watch them both together even with a butt call. That was some special ACT RIGHT PROBLEM SOLVED.

Josephine and Joe were having a great day. Then Josephine said to Joe do you love me Joe? He YES, I always love you. Josephine well I love you and we have our children, we have a dog. Then Josephine said the only thing missing is that we're not married, Joe said everything is so good. I never thought about it, so they call Bruce Leroy. They told him the problem. He said I'm on the way. He get there and said I don't have any Act right for this. But I know God Has some SUPER ACT RIGHT. Then puff a Preacher pop up, and organist, then puff a big church, then all their friends. It's magic; they were married. Then Bruce Leroy said one more thing. Here's free tickets to Hawaii for a week; everything is paid for. Josephine and Joe said thank you to Bruce Leroy. But what about the kids? Bruce Leroy said I will take care of them. I always have, so ACT RIGHT FOR KIDS problem solved again.

3.

Short Stories

Pimp Daddy's Car	32
Miss Big Butt	33
She was so sexy	34
If I was a DJ	35
Freebie (sex)	36
Aletha too cool	38
Cool Charles	39
Stay all night	40
Stay out of Jail	42

Pimp Daddy Car

Pimp daddy car was so sharp, he use to get ticket for going too slow because he had people walking beside it wiping the dust off when he was riding.

Pimp daddy car was so sharp, the only way to sit in it your clothes had to be brand new or just come out of the dry cleaners.

Pimp daddy car was so sharp, women would run behind him because when a woman get out they might get in.

Pimp daddy car was so sharp, he would get gas free because people would follow him to use the same gas he did.

Pimp daddy car was so sharp, it never broke down because the mechanic would get a freebie from his ladies whenever he had to get a tune up.

Pimp daddy car was so sharp, he would take it when he went out of town. They asked him why it had such low mile age. Because he have it ship in advance so it would be there when he get there. So when they see him drive up they would say it's Pimp Daddy; it's time to party.

Miss Big Butt

Her butt was so big, when she walks in the room, the room would shake.

Her butt was so big, when she walk through a door she had to turn side ways.

Her butt was so big, the men would follow her thinking they would get a butt call.

Her butt was so big, her shake was so pretty men wanted to suck it like a milk shake.

Her butt was so big, when she was walking down the side walk, the police would stop traffic so no one would not have a car wreck.

Her butt was so big, she had to sleep in two king's size beds.

Her butt was so big, to get in car they had to bring back the Kissing doors on her convertible truck.

Her butt was so big, when she went to the club, she had four men when she dance. Each man had his own spot beside her.

She Was So Sexy

She was so sexy, she had a lot of Jobs, but did not have to go because her bosses made house calls.

She was so sexy, never had to go out for anything because the delivery man always get a freebie (sex).

She was so sexy, all her clothes were snap on, so they would be easy to pop off.

She was so sexy, and always in great shape, because she would work out in any position her men wanted.

She was so sexy, her car never broke down because her mechanic always made house calls got a freebie (sex) for her tune ups.

She was so sexy and did not have many girlfriends, because when the girl did not know where the husbands or boyfriends were, they know where they was not supposed to be.

She was so sexy, that when she walk down the sidewalks the police had to stop traffic because men could not keep their eyes on the road.

if i Was a DJ

If I was a DJ, I would play music that would make you want to dance forever, but only at the clubs. That's right, that's right, till the break of dawn.

If I was a DJ, I would play love songs at night that make you sleepy so you could get to work on time, and the ladies that come to the clubs would be all mine.

If I was a DJ, I would play music for the kids that would make them smart and work good things in their heart.

If I was a DJ, I would make a song you could play to make someone fall in love with you every day.

If I was a DJ, there will always be a time you could tell me what to play except when I'm getting a freebie. That right, that right, you can do it all night.

If I was a DJ, I would make a dance that you could do that would fit every song that everyone could do.

If I was a DJ, I would make a holiday that you could take off work and party all day every month on Friday. That's right, that's right and do it all night.

If I was a DJ, there would be a day on the radio that all your greatest hits will be play for 24 and it would be on a Saturday. That's right, that's right and you can party all night.

If I was a DJ, I would ROCK the Universes. That's right, that's right we can do it all night.

The Freeby

What is a freebie (sex)?

When a man has sex with women and does not have to pay for it. When a woman have sex with a man and does not have to pay, that is called a freebie (sex).

She has a good running car and don't have to pay for a tune up; she gives her mechanic a freebie.

John always in good health because, when he gets a checkup, he gives the Doctor a freebie.

They say she always get days off whenever she wants to, because she gives the boss some freebies.

How can she afford those expensive clothes and work at the Family Dollar? She gives her expensive clothes salesman freebies.

What make your cable bills so cheap and you get all the stuff Comcast offer? Her cable man gets a lot of freebies.

How come every Super Bowl she gets tickets and good seats? The Coaches of the teams each get freebies.

Is a freebie good or bad? Good if she's pretty; bad if she's ugly.

If a woman wants a freebie, what do they have to do? Just find a man she wants and say I want a freebie, and it's on to the break of dawn.

Will they ever stop the freebies in this world? Only when they gone out of sex.

Is freebie only for sex? No it also for butt calls.

Can you get a freebie on the internet? YES, only if you have a good hand of up and down, or a good hand of left and right.

How can you get a freebie every day? Easy just win the Powerball and the freebies will come to you and the butt calls too.

A freebie what the best place to get a freebie? If you're not a regular it is impossible.

Have freebies been going on very long? If you have a long one you should know.

You never hear about people getting freebies. If you were getting one, would you tell?

After you get a freebie can you get another? YES, for half price.

Freebies, freebies, freebies, that's all people are talking about. What's wrong with that, haven't you got one lately?

Aletha Too Cool

Aletha was so cool, the clothes she wore came to her before they got in the stories in the town she lived in, so she could wear them first.

Aletha was so cool, when she went out the guys stood in line to see where she went so they could be close to her at all times.

Aletha was so clean to go in her house you had to put on sunglasses, because the house was so clean it shined like the sun.

Aletha cooked so good just the smell of her food made people hungry.

Aletha, her clothes were so fly that people would ask what plant did this come from.

Aletha, her car was so sharp that the people always asked her where they can buy one.

Aletha was so cool, her pets had a butler and a maid.

Aletha was so cool, when she went out of town, when she show up, everyone says Althea here, let's get this party started, and damn she's sharp.

The Coolest Charles Of Charleses

Charles was so cool, when Charles said what's up, all the ladies said, Me, Me; some say All of Me.

Charles was so sharp, that everyone would follow him around to buy what he bought to look like him.

Charles was so clean, that the ladies had to take off their clothes at the door to come in his house.

Charles could cook so good, that he hardly got to eat it because everyone was always in line for what he cooked.

Charles could hoop so good that he could shoot long shots blindfolded.

Charles car was so sharp, that when it rained people would hold umbrellas over it to keep it from getting wet.

Charles cash was so strong he did not have to pay for anything or use a credit card; he just signed his name.

Charles pets were so cool, the dog did not bark loud; it just showed the grill of his teeth; the cat did not meow, it just meeed.

Charles was so cool, wherever he went they would roll up the red carpet, and tell the DJ, here comes Charles; this party is on, damn he's sharp.

Stay All Night

To stay all night what is that?

When a man and a women sleep together and live in different places, but don't, and have sex over and over and over to the break of dawn, that's a stay all night.

Can a man sleep over with a woman? YES, as long as he's out before her husband or boyfriend gets home.

Can a stay all night be good or bad for a man? Good if the woman is pretty and bad if a woman is ugly.

What make you want to stay all night? Because it's better than a butt call.

If you want a woman to stay all night, tell her she will get breakfast in bed in the morning. It will work 50% of the time.

Stay all night, can it be fast or slow? Fast if it's quick sex; slow is great. That's long slow sex.

Stay all night in the club is when you hook up with a lady. Get her a lot of drinks, offer to take her home. Say you forgot something at your house then when you get there, say I will only be a minute. Offer some more drinks then she will stay all night.

If you stay all night does that mean you get a lot of sleep? HELL no!

What all goes on with staying all night? If you do it right you make love, breakfast in bed, and maybe a butt call.

Will staying all night be good thing or bad thing? If you wake up and your lady is pretty it's good; if you wake up and your lady is ugly that's bad.

After and you stayed all night and you want to do it again make sure that he or she is not married or have a boyfriend or girlfriend.

If there is a couple that hooked up for a staying all night, if you can't go home, get a hotel room for a quickie.

Every time you stay all night it gets crazy next time. Get the right one babieee.

I have never had a good date to stay all night, and then you better try staying all day.

Every time I do the stay all night I end up cooking. The next time pick up some take out to take in – problem solve.

If you're having fun when you stay all night, how come you have to go? Because it's stay all night not stay all day.

How would you know when you bring home someone to stay all night they will not steal from you? Just keep your eyes on them.

Stay Out Of Jail

To stay out of jail, don't commit a crime and get caught. Do crime; do the time.

To stay out of jail, never tell someone you're going to rob something and do it where they work.

To stay out of jail, never look in the camera in the place you're committing the crime your chose. Smile if you do.

To stay out of jail, never ask where you are going to court if you committed a crime and get caught.

To stay out of jail, never commit a crime and tell your ex-wife if you have married again.

To stay out of jail, you commit a crime, get caught, make bond.

To stay out of jail, never tell a friend you owe money to you are going to rob a bank and get away with it but don't pay them back.

To stay out of jail, do not go in Wal-Mart bag up your own products to go out the door without a receipt. It does not work; they have door checkers. No receipt no out.

To stay out of jail, stay at home.

To stay out of jail, never drink alcohol and drive. Drink alcohol at home, or don't drink at all.

To stay out of jail, if you steal, you'll get caught. If you sell it, you'll get caught. If you pawn it, you'll get caught. If you got it, you'll get caught.

To stay out of jail, never commit a crime and go back to the same place to do it again unless you want to get caught.

To stay out of jail, if you steal car make sure it has gas in it, and don't take it home.

To stay out of jail, if you rob a bank, make sure you have plan it. Before you rob it, make sure you have a car that will not break down.

To stay out of jail, if you are about to have sex, you're about to stick it in, and the girl says NO, then you stop. Right, no don't means yes.

To stay out of jail, if you are in need of money, the store on the corner can easily be robbed. They will give you the money, but the camera will get it back.

To stay out of jail, never break into a house that says beware of the dog. You go in the house, the dog does nothing; you get what you want, the dog is watching and still does nothing, but when you get ready to go, the Rottweiler says he want to play for a while. Roof Roof.

4.

Things People Deal With in Life

Power ball	45
Airplane Trips	47
Jobs	49
Bills	51
Rent, Rent, and More Rent	53
Cash Money Dollar Bills Yawl	55
Gas, Gas and More Gas	57
Sleep, Sleep and More Sleep	59
Cold Sick Cold	62

Power Ball

Why should I play power ball? One to be a millionaire, two pay off all my bills, three win to get a lot of butt calls.

Power ball is it gambling? Yes and No; if you lose yes; if you win no.

Have anyone you know won? No, most of the time the people that win they just disappear.

As the years go by, what is good about power ball? You can always want to win; maybe I will win this time.

After you spent so much money and never won, what would you do? Play double power ball winning get better.

Will it get better in any way to win? YES, just look if you don't play, you can't win. Winners never quite.

Play power ball, the people play; one wins. That is the rule. What if a lot of people win? That could be a problem.

Win, win, win that's what they always say. They say lose, lose, lose when they don't win most of the time.

I what to win. OK this is what you do. Give your money to someone else; let them play for you. If you lose blame them.

How can you win on power ball? Play until you win or run out of money whichever comes first.

What is the best way to play power ball? Playing the numbers that did not fall already.

Can every one win YES, just one at a time?

Is it ok to play it a lot? YES, you can play all you want until you get broke.

Does it take a long time to win the power ball? NO, your chance of winning is every time, but don't bet on it.

When is the best time to play power ball? Before you get paid. If you play when you get paid you'll be broke again.

The money you spend on playing power ball, do you ever get it back? If you don't win, one way if you know someone that has won, ask them for a loan. Then you got a lead on the same winning numbers.

Power ball is a game; how much should I spend on it? Only the amount that you don't need. Your chance to win is a million to one.

Airplane Trips

If you're going on airplane trip do you tell everyone? NO, tell them when you get back so your house won't get broken into.

Is it ok to fly in an airplane? YES, only if you know that the plane will take off and land, will not cash, catch fire in the air or run off the runway taking off. If that won't happen it's not OK.

Are all planes safe? YES and NO, a good plane will get you there; a bad plane will just disappear.

Will it be good to go on a plane and Jump out? YES, as long as you have a parachute and land on land and not in water.

What is good about taking a plane trip? You get food, free drinks and if you're lucky you can meet nice people going where you're going and you get a butt call.

Can you go around the world? YES, if you have a lot of pilots, a lot of gas, a lot of people to go and a company crazy enough to pay for it.

Why does it take so long to get on a plane? Security has to check you in; your luggage has to be checked for weapons and to make sure that you are not taking anything that will be too big.

If your plane crashes do you get a refund? YES, only if you were on the plane.

If you were going on a trip and you're on the plane. It's about to take off; you change your mind. How do you get off? You don't HA HA.

Airplane trip – if you're going on airplane trip your flight leaves at 10:00am you need to be there at 7:00am just to go through security.

Airplane trip – if you in a plane and you meet someone don't tell them your address while in the air. They could break in your house.

Airplane trip – when you are going out of town make plans ahead of time for a good hotel, so when you get where you're going you won't be in an old run down hole in the wall with bugs big enough to say what's up.

Airplane trip – if you're going to another country get a book to help translate the language, so you don't say hello and in that country it means let's have sex.

Airplane trip – when you're in the air and the plane starts to shake, don't fall apart; its only air clouds not that we're going to crash.

Airplane trip – after your plane lands and you're in another country, never go with the first person that comes to you, being so super nice. You could end up held for ransom.

Airplane trip – if your plane is about to take off and you're not on board and a thunder storm starts, don't go.

Jobs

Jobs can make your life or break your life, because you have to work.

Jobs – can; you fall in love on your job? YES, if you don't get fired for sexual harassment.

Jobs – can you get rich with your jobs? YES, if you want to starve to death, it will take you that long to save the money.

Jobs – is a good job hard to find NO, unless you got a felony, after felony, after felony.

Jobs – is it hard to keep a good job NO, only if you stay away from the boss's wife or husband.

Jobs – what jobs pay the most money? The one you get hired for.

Jobs – If you got married to someone at your job is that good or bad? Bad because no way you can fool around at work anymore.

Jobs – if you and your wife or husband, and she or he makes more money than you, is that good or bad? Good if he or she does. Then I can stay at home.

Jobs – if I get a good job are there ways to get a promotion? YES, send a lot of emails.

Jobs – are they all for educated people? NO, just for the one that apply online.

Jobs – have the time change to where the foreign people from other countries, get the good jobs? No *abbla espanyo*.

Jobs – can a person with a felony get a good job YES and NO. If it was a speeding ticket YES. If they were trying to get away from a bank robbery NO.

Jobs – will the new president help the black people get good jobs? They will be lucky if he helps them to get a job at all.

Jobs – do all jobs get tax refunds? YES and NO. If you get a check YES. If you get paid cash NO.

Jobs – have the world got too hard for a convict to get a good job? NO, they just follow them when they work with a shotgun.

Jobs – I think it's totally unfair why if they're not in jail and free why they being watched with shotgun. Because all jobs handle money.

Bills

Bills – will bills ever stop being bills? YES, when your six feet under.

Bills – can a bill ever pay a bill? YES, when you give the bill collector a freebie (sex).

Bills – can a bill ever be free? YES; only if you never start one.

Bills – can a bill ever be around and not cost money? YES, when that's your name, Mr. Bill.

Bills – is there a country that don't have bills? YES, on Mars; we haven't got up there yet.

Bills – what is the cheapest bill you can pay? The one that don't take your whole check.

Bills – if you can't pay your bills what will happen Your bill will turn into a night mare.

Bills – what does all bills have in common? They all keep coming and coming and coming and coming until you die.

Bills – a bill that has been paid and it keeps coming what should I do to get rid of it? Just pay the next one.

Bills – what bill can be a bill that you don't have to pay? A child named Bill.

Bills – can I pray to God to stop my bills? YES, although God won't be the one the collectors are looking for.

Bills – are all bills to be paid with cash? NO, credit cards are ok as long as the card belongs to you, and not to anyone else.

Bills – will all my bills come at the same time? NO, they can be arranged any way you like as long as they get paid, and you can't say you don't want them to come all.

Bills – if your bills keep coming when you die, just tell them God will tell them about the bills – problem solved.

Bills – my bills have been over paid what can I do? Be happy it was not late.

Bills – if your bills goes to the collection agency where can you go to get a loan to pay it? Any where they have money that you don't have to pay back.

Bills – do rich people have to have to pay bills? No, they are the people you have to pay your bills to.

Rent, Rent and More Rent

Rent – is rent good or bad? Its good if you're the renter its bad if you're the rentee.

Rent – what is good to rent? Anything you can rent and get paid for it.

Rent – can you rent people? YES, as long as it legal labor.

Rent – can you rent kids? YES, as long as they do the work at home.

Rent – Can you rent your pets? YES, as long as you sign if you get bit I'm not responsible contract.

Rent – how can you get a lot of stuff to rent? If you have a credit card Amazon can mail it to you ASAP.

Rent – what if you rent someone something and they don't bring it back? You call Bruce Leroy; give him the address. He will find them and give them some Act right – problem solved.

Rent – can you rent something and get it free? YES, if you pay for it with a freebie (sex).

Rent – if you live in a house can you rent it to someone else? YES, as long as the renter pays the rentee, and the rentee pays the other renter.

Rent – is the renting business good for everyone? YES, just rent something, pay for it, and rent it to someone else.

Rent – how often can you rent something? When you need it, rent it or after you get paid rent it. Rent just rent, rent, rent, rent.

Rent – do you need a lot of money to rent? YES and NO. If you have a lot of money rent something good. If you have a little money just rent.

Rent – after you rent something is it ok to pay it off? YES, just don't rent the same thing again.

Rent – after everything is a rented off what can you do? Call Amazon and buy some more and rent, rent, rent.

Rent – can you rent movies? YES, if you have not watched it.

Rent– will renting ever go out of style? YES, when people run out of money.

Rent – Can you rent an Island? YES, if you own a country.

Rent – can you rent the world? YES, if you own the Galaxy.

Cash Money—Dollar Bills Y'all

What is cash money?

It is the money that you make to live your life, until it's all gone.

Cash money, can you get me a husband? YES, just get on Facebook, say you want a man and they don't have to work, but don't mention you have five kids.

Cash money, can you get me a house? YES, just find a house but don't put my name of the lease.

Cash Money, can you bail me out of jail? YES, just call the bondsman, tell them you got cash money, although they will have to find me to pay for you.

Cash money, can you get me a good job? YES, just find the job you want; tell them cash money sent you, just make sure you're not working for free.

Cash money, can you get me a trip to Los Vegas? YES, just get on the plane, stay in the restroom until the plane takes off, but you have to find your own way back.

Cash money, can you take me out for dinner? YES, go to the restaurant, order your food, have a good meal, just don't use my name.

Cash money, why do you always have so much money? Because I never pay for anything.

Cash money, can you make me rich? YES, get a job or do a lot of begging.

Cash money, can you pay my bills? YES, just write them on a check, but don't give them my name.

Cash money, can you get me a car? YES, go to a car lot and take a test drive, but it's not my fault you didn't come back.

Cash money, can you get me a wife? YES, just get on the internet, say you're rich, but when she shows up tell her you're still waiting on your inheritance.

Cash money, can you help me win the Powerball? YES, just keep playing until I say stop.

Cash money, can you help the Titans win the Super Bowl? YES, get Coach Fisher back.

Cash money, can you help me to get into outer space? YES, just find some aliens and catch a ride.

Gas, Gas, And More Gas

What is gas?

It's what we put in cars, buses, trucks, planes. It is something that cost more than money.

Gas, can I do without gas? YES, if you like walking.

Gas, can gas ever be replaced? YES and NO. Yes if you will pay a hundred thousand for an electric car. No I'll keep my huupty.

Gas, will we ever run out of gas? If we do, get a job close to home.

Gas, can gas be dangerous? YES, only if you light a match while pumping it.

Gas, if you're going on a long trip how can you save on gas? Don't go.

Gas, is it easy to save on gas? YES, when it's time to go, don't. When you feel like going, don't. When they say it's time to go, just say I already been.

Gas, where can you find cheap gas? When you run out the closest one is the best one.

Gas, gas, gas. Is there something better to talk about? YES, a fill up.

Gas, flying cars. If they ever get them made will there still be gas? NO, it won't be liquid gas; it will be electric gas.

Gas, if you could get gas for free what would you do? Get all I can and sell it.

Gas prices was so high I had to ride the bus to work and wait to drive my car on the weekend.

Gas prices was so high, I could not buy lunch on the week days so I could go shopping on the weekend.

Gas was only in one place in our town so I had to move in town instead of living out of town.

Gas was so high that me and my neighbor he drive to work a week then I drive to work a week. It got so our wives did it also. They liked it because they just went shopping.

Gas at one time was so short in supply in our town I made money selling my gas when I was not going anywhere for double the price.

Gas has always been the most important material in our town. We had to vote do we want the water pump fix or the gas pump fix? They voted for the gas pump. Everyone had to drink bottled water.

Gas, is it better to save on gas with a new car or an old car? An old car is cheaper it don't have a car note.

Sleep, Sleep And More Sleep

What is sleep

It is the formation of your body, with your eyes closed in bed with your body resting and no one is bugging you.

Doctor Sleep, can you help me to wake up on time for work? Sometimes I just sleep for days. YES, buy five alarm clocks. Set them for different times to go off away from your bed. By the time the last one goes off, you will be woke; then go to work.

Doctor Sleep, what can I do for my kids? I send them to bed on time, but they never want to get up for school. Here is what you do. As soon as they get home from school, make them get in bed. They will say we want to go out and play and watch TV and eat dinner. Will you get up on time for school? They all will say YES – problem solved.

Doctor sleep, I work so hard on my job but I have hard time going to sleep. What kind of job do you have, over the phone computer repair man? Well here is what you do. When you get home from work walk around you block three times. Then find a little house work to do. Then have a good dinner. If you're not sleepy by then take a sleeping pill.

Doctor sleep, my husband is a good man. We have great sex, but his snoring is so loud I can't sleep even if he's in the other room. I miss sleeping with him. What can I do? This is what you do. Try to put him in a sleeping position that he will not snore. If that don't work, try ear plugs. If that don't work, try sleeping pills. If that don't work, you married the wrong man.

Doctor Sleep, I have a problem. My son is still wetting his bed. How old is he? 10 years old. Try this. Don't let him drink anything after 7:00 pm and make sure he eats his bread and vegetables at dinner. Make sure he uses the rest room two times before he goes to sleep. If that don't work, call Bruce Leroy. He will give him some Act Right.

Doctor sleep, my girlfriend is so afraid of flying. She hates to take pills. We're going to Hawaii. The only way to get there is by plane. What can I do? Here is what you do. Tell here the Doctor told me what to do for you. This will solve your problem, a powerful solution. Give it to the airline stewardess drop it in her drink. Then tell her we're going to celebrate the trip. She will bring you the drinks. She will drink it and be out like a light. I will send you the bill.

Doctor Sleep, every time I and my husband go on a trip all he does is sleep, most of the time. This time I want him up so we can have fun together and take pictures, do videos and all that stuff. This is what you do. Two weeks before the trip, tell him you're not feeling well for sex and the Doctor said you have to be in great shape. Tell him on the trip you can have a lot of butt calls.

Doctor Sleep, I have to watch over my mother; she walks in her sleep. There are steps everywhere in my house. We moved her bedroom down stairs, but there are still a few steps down stairs. What can I do? First get some light sensors on each side of the bed. When she get up and step into the light, it will buzz and let you know. Then you can tend to her. Doctor Sleep the sensors are working fine, but now instead of walking, now she's running in her sleep.

Doctor Sleep, how can I get my kids to go to sleep at the right time, so they can get up and go to school at the right time. Call Bruce Leroy he will give them Act Right – problem solved.

Doctor Sleep, my son is a great kid. He go to sleep on time, get up on time to go to school on time, but they say he still sleeps in class. Ask him if you will stop sleeping in class or should I call Bruce Leroy? He said he'll stop sleeping in class and will Act Right.

Cold, Sick, Cold

What is a cold?

It is a sickness. You have a runny nose, you sneeze a lot, you cough a lot, and you're tired, and you get everyone else sick too.

Mr. Cold, if I'm getting married tomorrow, how I can get rid of a cold? First you go to a pharmacy; get all the medicine they have to get rid of colds; take them all. If you wake up, you'll feel great. Congratulations.

Mr. Cold, I have six children and they all came down with a cold. First get a big pot for chicken soup; chop them up a lot of chicken. Give them all Tylenol for children's cold. Let them eat and drink the soup, stay in bed and eat, drink the soup for 24 hours. They will be OK if that works. If that don't work, Call Bruce Leroy to give them Get You Sick Act Right.

Doctor Cold, we have a lot of children coming to school sick with a cold, what can we do? Make some calls to the Governor tell him we are going to need some food stamps for a lot of chicken soup to save the school children.

Mr. Cold, I just heard on the news that half of the people in the United States has got a cold. What can we do? First of all, it is not true if you just got it from the internet news. You just got hacked by the kids. They just don't want to go to school. It's time for exams and they did not study.

Mr. Cold, when will we stop having colds? That will happen when people stop kissing, doing the nasty, and kids start eating their vegetables. We might have a chance then.

Mr. Cold, when will children stop playing sick so they won't have to go to school? What can we do? When you tell them you're going to call Bruce Leroy to give them some Act Right, no more problem.

Mr. Cold, no one likes to get a cold. What can we do? Don't get sick.

Mr. Cold, every year colds get worse. What can we do? First of all, are you sick? NO. Have you been sick? NO. Do you want to get sick? NO. – problem solved.

Mr. Cold, my mother has a special home remedy for colds. Do every one know about it? NO. Do she give it to everyone? NO. Can you make it? NO. It's the one I gave her.

Mr. Cold, they say the flu only last 48 hours, but the cold last longer. What is the problem? The truth is the flu is only half a cold.

Mr. Cold, every year this time of the year I get a cold. What can I do to solve the problem? Well let's see; how do you feel now? I feel great. Well problem solved no cold.

Mr. Cold, they say that every year you should get a flu vaccination; it's a shot. What if people don't take the shot? Tell them to hang around the people that took the shot. They won't get sick so the people that hang around them won't get sick ether – problem solved.

Mr. Cold, I'm sick with a cold, can you help me? Hey Mr. Cold where are you going? Away from you, you're sick; text me. I'll text you back on what you can do. I don't want to get sick like you.

5.
All About The Weather

Rain, Rain, and More Rain	65
Thunder, Thunder with Thunder	68
Lightning, Lightning, Too Much Lightning	71
Clouds, Big Clouds, and Bigger Clouds	74
Tornado, Tornado, What Tornado?	77
Hurricane, Hurricane, Bad Hurricane	80
Earth Quake, Earth Quake, & Earth Quake	83

Rain, Rain, and More Rain

What is rain?

It is the liquid that comes from the sky. They call it rain and God used it to make the ocean. People use it to catch colds.

The rain is a great thing. It makes the crops grow, makes your grass grow. Sometimes if you don't have a lawnmower your grass could get so high, your house will look like a farm.

Rain comes down from the sky, then it comes down from the mountains , then it come down to the creeks, then it comes down to the river. Then too much rain it could take your house with it.

Rain is good for children to play in, in the summer time. In the winter they play in the rain but it is snow. What happens in the meantime? Most people caught in the house with a cold.

When do you know the rain is going to come? On the T.V. the news weather man tell us. Sometimes they're right; sometimes they're wrong. In the summer time you take you're umbrella. If it rains you're ready. If it don't, it can keep that 100 degree hot sun off you – problem solved again.

What's the best thing about rain? It's free.

What happens if it doesn't rain for a very long period of time? Buy bottled water.

What happens if I get caught in a bad, bad rain storm? What should I do? One pray to God that it stops; two pray that God hears you this time.

Rain is a greatest liquid in the world, because the water helps to make liquid. When liquid does not have water, in it gas.

I love it when it rains and I'm at home and it's Saturday. It makes me sleepy and I'm sleeping so good. Now it's Sunday and it's still raining. Monday and it's still raining. Tuesday it can stop raining now I've had enough sleep.

All people in the world get rain. Does America get rain, and do they get American rain? Does Mexico get rain, and do they get Mexican rain? No. It does not work like that. Tennessee don't get Tennessee rain. Atlanta doesn't get Atlanta rain. Let's just say that the world get world rain.

If it rain for forty days and forty nights, will that ever happen again? NO, we're lucky if we get two days of rain.

What happen if it stops raining for forty days and forty nights? I think they're writing another Bible.

I love to watch it rain in the window. Then all of a sudden, cars start floating by. That means tell your mother we got a problem.

Is rain good or bad? It's good when it rains. The little flowers grow, and they're pretty, and the sun comes back out, but it's bad when it don't rain at all.

Rain, rain, go away; little Eric want to play. So the rain stops. Now here comes a big storm; now go play in that, HA HA.

If you live in London, England, where it rains all the time and they have lot of fog, what could you do? Just e-mail the Queen, and have her talk to Mother Nature.

What's up with rain and snow? It's like this. When it rain it get made into snow, so in the summer we have to make the rain very happy. It could turn on us. Rain is the power for the water of the world. Thank God for the rain, but you hold off the tornado, the hurricane and the snow. For the rain not too much this time. P. S. the last flood my house floated across the street.

Thunder, Thunder With Thunder

What is thunder?

It is a super loud sound you hear when it rains, storm, tornadoes and hurricane, and please don't forget the sound your mother makes when you do something she told you not to do.

Thunder – you hear it when a heavy storm is about to come, or when the sound of your daddy makes when you use up all the gas in his car.

Thunder – you will always hear when a tornado is about to come, or the sound your girlfriend makes when she see you with another women.

Thunder is always loud when a hurricane comes. It also comes when your husband comes home early and find you in the bed with another man. You'll hear his thunder.

If you ever had an alarm clock that never got you up on time, thunder its worse. It's so loud it won't even let you sleep.

Some people say the people next door make thunder when they make love. Their head board on their bed hits wall so hard it wakes up the neighborhood.

I like thunder because girlfriend get horrified of it so when it starts to rain and thunder I say, well it's raining. Think I will go home. Then she says no please stay. Then

I'll say you going to give me some? YES, YES, YES. Then I know it's going to be a butt call.

Rains bring the thunder or do the thunders bring the rain? Let's just call it here comes the weather.

Is thunder the loudest sound in the world? Not really. I heard a fat lady fart; it was so loud it shook the whole room.

Thunder can be bad when it wants to be, and it can be good when it wants to be. A man was breaking into a house, and the thunder came and the window fell on him, and that made him get caught in the window, and a dog bit him in the ass – problem solved.

Thunder is so loud that the sound can't even be recorded. They cannot get the timing right, they turn on recorder. It would not catch the thunder, and then they turn the system back on no thunder. So they got another system. They tried another system. Thunder, lightning, more thunder. System blow out electrical – big problem.

Some people say the thunder it is the Greek gods having a conversation. They said we need more butt calls. These butt calls don't have enough Thunder.

All thunder is not bad thunder. We named or dog Thunder. It's a Rottweiler. When we call him, people always think we're trying to make it rain.

After a good, good rain the sun comes out and it keeps on thundering. Men say that means they should get a free butt call.

All thunder never sounds the same. You have quiet thunder and loud thunder. Is the super thunder the one that comes and you don't get rain? It just get you confused.

I love the weather. You can always get to see the weather report and know what is going to happen. They never say anything about the thunder. Sometimes the thunder can be so loud that you will stop what you're doing except a butt call.

I believe thunder is a very strong power. It is so loud that people look up to see what's is going to happen. If the thunder get louder, louder and louder, get the hell away from where you are. God is mad at someone.

Lightning, Lightning, Too Much Lightning

What is lightning?

It is the beam of light in the sky that comes with rain, tornadoes, hurricanes, and they also call moonshine white lightning.

Lightning comes in heavy weather and light weather. You know it was there when you see a tree that is cut half in two with a black burn mark on it. That was lightning or someone was out camping.

People are so afraid of lightning, although when seen it has such beauty until you see what it hit. It hit the girl. She's fine except when she eat or drinks, everything lights up.

They say that lightning won't give us electricity, then why whenever we have a big storm light goes out?

Lightning is one of scientist biggest question. Where does it come from? A lot of people say when we have the big storm why doesn't it just stay up there.

There is other lightning, as fast as greased lightning, and my Uncle Eric make some shine that strong as lightning. My niece Victoria got struck by lightning. She doesn't have to pay an electric bill. She can light up her house and charge all her batteries.

Lightning comes with the weather, so two things you don't do. One don't hold metal in the rain or stand in water in the lightning. It will attract lightning, and it will be glad to meet you.

Lightning, lightning, where did you come from and how long have you been around? God made this world so do the right thing in life. You can ask God what He want you to do, so if you shock someone it has to feel good. AMEN.

Lightning, lightning where you been? Lightning said I went up town then I went down town. When you going back? Can't say; they not there no more.

A man said he was plowing and planting his crop. Mr. Lightning came along and the man said I see you and hear all that thunder. When we are going to get some rain? Mr. Lightning said we're trying to wake Mrs. Rain up.

Some people say they love to see the lightning, so they asked Mr. Lightning, when will we see lightning? Is the sound thunder different? YES, you hear thunder, but you can see and hear my Lightning, and when it strike you'll know it.

Mr. Lightning, why are you so powerful? Mr. Lightning said they're so many bad people in the world so I have to get rid of some of them. How do you do that? See those people running? They're on the list.

Mr. Lightning we see on T.V. that when people are dying they put them on a machine on their heart to bring them back alive. Can you do that? Well the truth is I told them how to do that.

Mr. Lightning, people are going into outer space. Is there lightning in outer space? How do you think the Aliens got to earth?

Mr. Lightning, what make you so special? God said let there be light. I've been here every since.

Mr. Lightning, is there a Mrs. Lightning? Yes, when you see lightning and there is no rain that means we're having a party. When you hear thunder we're opening Champaign. When you see the rain, the D.J. just put on James Brown. That's how lightning party.

Clouds, Big Clouds and Bigger Clouds

What is a cloud?

It's a beautiful thing in the sky that is fluffy. It can be white, blue, grey or brown, a great ray of colors, and from it we get rain, thunder, lightning the total production of weather, and on a special day you'll get a rainbow.

Mr. Cloud, are you good or bad? I'm good on a beautiful day nice clouds. A bad day means you have made me mad, and I will rain on you all day.

They say clouds go all the way around the world. Not really; we hang where the ladies look good so we can see them do their butt calls.

Mr. Cloud, we see that all the time. Ladies fly in planes, leg's hanging out the window of planes trying to give use a freebie.

Mr. Cloud, what do you do about the weather? I call lightning; he will text thunder; rain handles the internet, so you get a good tropical throw down; might leave you a rainbow.

Mr. Cloud, why do you have so many shapes? Because so many people are looking at me. I have to give them what they like to see. Sometimes I look like them.

Mr. Cloud, is there ever a time where the whole world can see you all at the same time? We tried that once, but it was too dark on one side of the world, so we just sent them videos of the clouds that was on the other side of the world.

Mr. Cloud, what is your favorite time of the year? Summer time is the time when ladies lay around with nothing on. Why do you like that? Because they are laying in the sun with nothing on. You've heard of drive bys, these are look bys, and we don't go by. For us it's a stay by.

Clouds, lightning, thunder and rain how do you work together to do the weather? When one of us is on break then the rest of us do a little extra.

Mr. Cloud, how we can get rain without clouds? You get a bucket of water and throw it up in the air and make believe it's raining. It might work out, because you will get wet.

Mr. Cloud, how can we see you at night when it rains? Mr. Lightning takes care of that; the lightning flashes you can see the clouds. The thunder will tell you where to look.

Mr. Cloud, does cloud change? Only when one goes on break.

Mr. Cloud, is there a Mrs. Cloud? Yes, most of the time she's out watching the rain.

Mr. Cloud, do you ever get tired of raining? Not really, because when the water comes back up it goes right back down.

Mr. Cloud, does thunder and lightning get along? YES, they have a great relationship. With no thunder you have no lightning; with no lightning you have no thunder, now you got rain.

Mr. Cloud, what season is the hardest for you? Winter. That's when I gain a lot of weight and my water turns into snow.

So as the world turns that was the CLOUD'S STORY.

… Eric Marton Cunningham

Tornado, Tornado, What Tornado?

What is a tornado?

It is a massive destructive force that comes in the weather and destroys everything in its path.

Mr. Tornado, why do you destroy everything in your path? I just walk and have big feet.

Mr. Tornado, what makes you come to the same places so much? I have friends in those places and we party a lot.

Mr. Tornado, is there a Mrs. Tornado? YES, most of the time she has her friends; they are in some places doing their own thing.

Mr. Tornado, every year around the same time you destroy most of the same things, in the same places. Why does that happen? You have to talk to my wife about that. That is where she always wants me to meet her, and I don't want her to be mad at me, so that where I go.

Mrs. Tornado, your husband MR. Tornado says you're the reason there are so many tornadoes in the same places every year. The travel agent give us the best discount on our vacation there. We'd go anywhere else if it was cheaper.

Mr. Tornado, why don't you give us a warning before you always have a lot of destruction? Well with the Thunder and Lightning doing their thing days ahead of time, most of the time we sleep late. They have to wake us up. That's why we get there so late. By that time the people should know we're coming.

Mr. and Mrs. Tornado, don't you take a break? Sometimes we do; every winter we go south and visit our friends Mr. and Mrs. Hurricane.

Big tornado or little tornado what is worse? The little ones; they are closer to the grown tornadoes.

Mrs. Tornado, what do you do in the tornado season mostly? I stay at home and watch my husband on the news.

Mr. Tornado, can't you do something good in the weather and not all that destruction? I would love to, but we get calls from people saying come tear this up; we need the money from insurance.

Mr. Tornado, is destruction all you know to do? Not really, moving is something me and my wife get calls for. Texas people want to move from the East, to the west, we take care of it.,Two years later they call and now they want to move back to where they were, so we give them what they call for. They just want to move, move and move.

Mr. Tornado, do tornadoes have times where they have two or three tornadoes in the same place? YES. How does that happen? We have a family reunion and everyone shows up and some be late and some be early, and that's how it happens.

Mrs. Tornado, who does the most destruction you or your husband? In the world today the equality has changed things. He stays at home with the kids in the summer no school, so in the summer my husband does a lot of work. He needs a break from all that spinning around; it wears him down.

Mr. and Mrs. Tornado, are all the years going to get better or worse? Well were getting old so were going to retire and let the children in the system. We have nine children and they are learning fast. Most of them have been out with their father a few times. They have some great round about moves and are in great shape.

Hurricanes, Hurricanes, Bad Hurricanes

What is a hurricane?

It is a part of the weather system that comes out of the ocean with a big round center that is called the eye. It's a storm with winds up to 150 miles an hour, waves of water 10, 20, 30 feet high. People move elsewhere until it's over.

Mr. Hurricane, what is it that makes you so mean? Well sometimes I just have a cold and all the wind that just a sneeze, and all the water is just clearing my throat.

Mr. Hurricane, your being tracked by radar. Why don't you just stay out there in the ocean? Well I have friends thunder and lightning. I have to come and see them; we have fun together.

Mr. Hurricane, why are you so destructive? Sometimes people call me. I have to give the people what they ask for. They say they want a new Island. Just clean this one out for us and they are insured. They get a new Island.

Mr. Hurricane, why do you hit the United States so hard? Well they never ask for much. They call for a few homes, new carpet and a few businesses; they don't ask for much. They just like to remodel a lot.

Mr. Hurricane, in the United States you wet the inland a very long way in, and went up the east coast all the way to New York. Well that was my fault. Me lightning and thunder we went on vacation, and my kids did the work. They did not read the e-mail.

Mr. Hurricane, what is the deal when you show up you have a different name? Well it's like this; when I travel under a different name, I get better discount from my travel agent.

Mr. Hurricane, what was the deal with New Orleans? That was so the people would get a lot of new stuff and win the Super Bowl. That's what they told me ahead of time, so I gave them what they asked for. They keep their part of the deal. They did win the Super Bowl and that's the story.

Mr. Hurricane, is there a Mrs. Hurricane? YES, but she just goes by Mrs. Tropical Storm. That what she's famous for. When I go in and get tired, she would finish up the job.

Mr. Hurricane, are all your names made by the same people? NO, they say they put a lot of names in a spinning wheel and pull one out, and that's what they call me, and that solves the problem.

Mrs. Tropical Storm, will your Husband Mr. Hurricane ever retire? YES. We have kids; after we name them all they will be taking his place. That's how it works. We'll get back to you on that.

Mr. Hurricane, have your work ever done any good? YES, YES, YES, all the new hotel, convention centers here on the Island. They were built after my demolition for it was under the contract paid in full. That's what the people asked for.

Mr. Hurricane, have any of you work been named after you? NO, I never take credit the names they give them. They get the famous on the news report; it's all in politics.

Mr. Hurricane, your life as a big hurricane King what has it done for you? As I go back to the places that I have been to, they look great like I never was there at all, so my kids will have something to do.

Earth Quake, Earth Quake, it's Earth Quake

What is an earth quake? It is an occurrences of the shaking of the earth in a massive form. That makes the earth open up cracks in places in the street, dirt, sidewalks, and buildings even fall. The sound is so loud, that there is nothing like it; once you hear it you will never forget it.

Mr. Earth Quake, where do you come from? I live in the center of the earth and it get so hot in there I just come up some times to work out and cool off, but sorry about my big feet. They knock thing over sometimes.

Mr. Earth Quake, why are you so loud? Well the elevator needs to be fixed, and they're too busy to get to it. So I have to use the stairs and it get on my nerves. I hit the walls sometimes; that's probably what you hear.

Mr. Earth Quake, we get giant waves from the ocean, from you pushing it in; we call it Tsunamis. That happens when I take a swim. After I work out I do a cannon ball off the high diving board. It's so refreshing and it feels great when I come back up to the surface.

Mr. Earth Quake, over in Europe they have very old historical buildings there. Why do you destroy them so much? I get calls that they want to rebuild. They didn't say when, so I just told them to send me an e-mail when they want me to take care of it, and that how it works.

Mr. Earth Quake, what up with the Volcanoes on the Islands and the one in the United States? Well what happened when it get so hot down here, I have turn my air conditioner or my AC unit outside. It pulls in the hot air and it goes up. I'm sorry about that but that is what happens.

Mr. Earth Quake, is there a Mrs. Earth Quake? YES, But she goes by Mrs. Tremlors. That's what she's famous for. When I show up and show out, when my show is over, she hangs around for a while for the grand finale.

Mr. Earth Quake, they say that the Arduous fault could sink California in the ocean. No, that my cousin; he get the hick ups a lot and the doctor says it will go away when the gets older – problem solved.

Mrs. Tremlors, when we get a lot of tremlors in California what's that all about? We do have friends over and we do that new Taiwan dance. It's a lot of fun and we even do it for hours. We got the top DJ that how we roll; that may be the problem.

Mr. Earth Quake, in the future will things get any worse? NO, when that AC unit was installed it's been so cool and comfortable we just take it easy. But we do still have the party's with the DJ.

Mr. Earth Quake, what's going on with St. Helens? That problem has only come up every 100 years, so we think she is cool for a good while; she is taking it easy – no more problems.

Mr. Earth Quake, is the United States safe form Earth Quakes? I'm out of shape now from our house party tremlors. I think we'll relocate for a few years, get in a condo, take time off with my wife, lose a few pounds and get into my wife's butt calls.

6.

About Animals

Family Pet	86
Birds	88
Dogs	90
Cats	92
Rabbits	94
Tigers	96
Lions	98
Cheetahs	100
Bears	102
Mountain Lions	104
Elephants	106
Rats	108
Squirrels	110
Pigeons	112
Eagles	115
Giraffes	118
Laughing Hyenas	121

Family Pet

What is a family pet?

It would be something everyone plays with, everyone feeds it and everyone cleans up after it. No let Mickey do it.

Family pet – if your dog barked at everyone that walked by, but one night your house was robbed while you were sleep would that be a good pet?

Family Pet – if you had a cat that only comes to you when it wants to, what would you do? Call it a lot of names and when it comes to me the name I called it that would be his name – problem solved.

If your kids wanted a pig for a pet would they get it? YES, but only if it was on a farm.

If your kids wanted a tiger for a pet could they have it? YES, if I was living in a jungle.

If your kids wanted a monkey for a pet could they have it? YES, if I was Tarzan and Jane.

If your kids wanted an Elephant for a pet? YES, if I had a circus.

If you're Kids wanted an Alligator for a pet could they have it? YES, if I was crazy.

If your kids wanted a Grizzly Bear? YES, but I would move out.

Family Pet – if you had a dog that goes over to the neighbor's yard to crap is that a good pet? YES, if you don't like your Neighbor.

Family Pet– if you had a pet fish and it ate meat and you were out and it jumped out the water after you, is that a good pet?

Family Pet – if your talking bird repeated everything you say and you and your wife had an argument. You walked away and said FU, and your bird kept saying it and your wife knew it was you who said it about her, would that be a good pet?

Family Pet – if your son had a Boa-constrictor and your daughter had a gerbil and the snake ate the gerbil while they were gone, would that be a good pet?

Family Pet – if you had an award winning show dog, black poodle and it had puppies and they came looking like mutts, would it be a good house pet or yard pet?

Family Pet – if your Kids brought home a cute little puppy and you decided to let them keep it and it grow up so big it eat you out of house and home, would that be a good pet?

Birds

What are birds?

The creatures that fly around and eat worms and breed and stuff and crap all over cars when you just washed it.

Are they good pets? If you want to clean their cage, get that tacky smell if you don't clean it and stay up all night if you're out of bird food and it's hungry, is that a good pet?

What is good thing about birds? They don't bark but they do tweet you to death.

Is it hard to train a bird? NO, it's impossible they are small creatures with small brains.

What is the best bird to buy for a pet? The one you can't afford.

Are birds safe for children? YES, if you keep them in a cage. No if plan training it to perform.

How do you name a bird? It easy call them a lot of names whichever one it responds to that would be the best name.

Is it ok to let birds fly around in your house? Yes if it's ok for them to crap on your stuff in your house.

Do birds fly all the time? NO, they stop to eat, and splash in water and crap on cars.

How can you catch a bird? Put out food, get a net and hide. You may catch one although a lot of them will attack you for the food.

Will birds get along with pets? Yes and no, dog yes, cat no. For a cat the bird will be its dinner if you don't feed the cat, when it get hungry.

If a bird flies into your house is it good luck or bad luck? It's good luck if it fly in; it's bad luck if you can't get it back out.

Can birds be hard to study? No, just find some and study them if you can keep up with them because the closer you get to them father away they will fly.

Can you eat birds? Yes and no, for a meal you need a hundred.

Birds, birds, birds are they all the same? Yes and no, there are a lot of kinds, but they look the same so good luck to find the type you want to study.

Do everyone like birds? Yes and No. No to the ones that have a lot of cats.

Dogs

What is a dog good for? A dog is man's best friend, if it doesn't bark all the time.

Are dogs good or bad? Good if you feed them, bad if you don't feed them they will bite you.

Can a dog help you if you need it? Yes, if you need help it can bark, roll over, and sit. If you need more then that you're out of luck.

Will dogs protect you? Yes, if your dog is bigger than your attacker. If not then you will have to protect your dog.

Is a big dog smarter than a little dog? Maybe if big dog is younger than the little dog. If the little dog is older it would be smarter than the big young dog – problem solved.

Are all dogs good pets? Yes, if they're bad call Bruce Leroy will give them some act right – another problem solved.

Is it hard to train a dog? No. You just send them to dog school.

How old do you have to be to get a dog? Old enough to buy food to feed it.

What can you train a dog to do? Hopefully not to bark all the time.

Do dog and cats get along? Yes and no, big dogs little cats no, big cat little dog maybe.

The history of dogs have they been around long? If you was hearing some barking they were around.

Can a dog be good for children? Yes, as long as you're going to feed it, clean up after it, keep its crap out of the neighbor's yard, and buy dog food, they are great for children.

Will a dog bite you? Yes, if the sign says "BE AWARE OF DOGS" then that dog will bite you and him and them any time.

Can people with dogs get along with people that have cats? YES and NO, if people come to your house and smell like a cat and you're dog smells it you will get a lot of bark, bark, bark. If people come to your house and smell like a dog and you have a cat they will get a lot of meows, meows, meows.

Are all dogs clean? Yes if you keep them out of the crap they make.

Are dogs good with other dogs? Yes, as long as it's a girl and boy dog and she's in heat.

Is it easy to name a dog? Yes, if it has spots then name it Spot.

Cats

What is a cat?

It is an animal that meows a lot, eats only what it likes, comes to you when it feel like it and is very clean. They always lay in your way.

What is good about a cat? It's not loud; it will not crap in your house and won't bark at everyone that comes to your house.

Can a cat be helpful? YES, if you are sleep they will wake you up only if they are hungry if there's no food in their bowl.

Are all cats the same? No, only the ones that wants to be the same.

Do cats get old? YES, very old. All they do is lay around, and lay around. When they die, they still lay around but they are not in your way.

How do you name a cat? You name him or her by what every they come to you by. Just call it a lot of names and whichever it comes to you by, give it that name.

Are cats fun? YES and NO, but when they're kittens they will play with anything, but when they get big they just lay around.

Can a cat be trained to do stuff? Yes: sit - no, roll over - no, fetch - no, be quit - meow.

Are all cats finicky? YES, only when you give them food they don't like, and be around people that smell like dogs.

Are birds safe around cats? YES, only when they can fly fast enough not to be dinner if the cat is hungry.

When a dog and cat live together who stays in the house? The one who is the cleanest.

After a kitten grows up to be a cat why they don't play? They don't bug you much; they lay around in the way all the time and look at you like you are crazy; that what cats do.

Are cats good at being left alone? YES, They just look out the window to see if you're gone and then they have a party.

Have cat been around long? YES, when you start hearing meows, meows, meows the cat was here.

If you have a lot of cats is that good? YES, you have a lot of cats you will never see any mice or rats.

Rabbits

What is a rabbit?

It is an animal. Some are wild; some can be pets. They have big long ears, big eyes, long hoppy feet to jump around all the time and eat up gardens.

Can a rabbit be good or bad? It can be good as a pet if you can train it, but it can be bad if you have a garden and it's wild. They love to eat.

Do Rabbits make people happy? YES, Bugs Bunny.

How big can a rabbit get? It can get as big as a dog if you feed it like a dog.

Are rabbits good for kids? Yes, when they are small and they're young, but when they get grown they will hop away to have sex and make baby rabbits.

How can you name a rabbit? Any name you like if they're in a cage If not when you put them down they will hop away. Call them any name. If it comes back, name it that name.

A rabbit is n animal that will trick you. If you play with them inside they're happy; if you play with them outside they're happier if you put them down. They like to play catch me if you can.

Hoppity, hoppity, hoppity that's what rabbits do. They don't bark; they don't meow; they just hop around and look at you like you crazy.

Will rabbits get along with dogs? YES and NO. Big dogs no; little dogs sometimes.

Can rabbits do tricks? If you train them to stay in the hat till you pull them out.

How can you train a rabbit? If you have a carrot and it's hungry, it will find you.

Do rabbits help save people? Only if they're covered with food, they can eat and bring them back to life so the people can see where they are.

Are rabbits here to stay? YES, for every two rabbits they can have HUNDREDS.

Is the rabbit species having any relatives? YES, the Kangaroo - it is a big, big, big rabbit.

A rabbit can always find food because what people throw away that's what they like to eat like especially, carrots, Big Macs, lettuces. They will fight for that.

Tigers

What is a tiger?

It is a wild super big kitty that is very powerful king of his land. It eats a lot so stay away when they are hungry or YOU COULD BE DINNER.

What is good about a tiger? It's very pretty in colors, and very clean; it never has any friends because when it's hungry they disappear.

Do tigers make good pets? Only when they're babies, but when they grow up, you're their pet.

Is a tiger good or bad? It's great when it's clean and feed, but when it's hungry it's like a Doctor Jeckle and Mr. Hyde.

Can a tiger be friendly? YES, they can be friendly until you see them lick their lips and look at you. Just run like HELL AND HOPE YOU GET AWAY.

Is it safe to be around tigers? YES, as long as you are in the other side of the cage.

If you see a tiger in the wild what should you do? If it did not see you run, run, I mean really run.

How can you name a tiger? Easy call it tiger; that is as close to them as you will get.

Tigers are so big one man will fill one up yum, yum.

What can they eat? If you was to feed one, it would cost your whole pay check.

How long do they stay small after birth? Just say you're feeding a very very, very big kitty cat.

Have tigers been around very long time? YES, when you heard about a big cat and every one was running from it, it was around.

Can you pet a tiger? YES and NO, you take your hand rub its back, you may be lunch.

After Tigers get put in cages and zoos what happens to the ones in the wild? If you find one, tell them.

The safest tiger in the world was Tony the Tiger for Frosted Flakes; he didn't bite.

Will there be a time when Tigers will be happy around people? YES, when they all are full of food and not hungry then its ok. That will last for 12 hours; then run, the tigers are hungry again.

Lions

What is a Lion?

It is a giant big kitty cat. It's light brown and the male has a big bushy fury head of hair, and when it roars you can hear it almost a mile away.

How can you know a lion is around? When all the other animals are running for dear life and you hear a sound and it makes the ground shake.

Where do Lions come from? Daddy lion get on momma lion and the do it cat style and make Lion babies.

What is good about a Lion? It is clean and it will never leave any dirty bones around.

Do Lions like to play? YES, they play with legs, your arms, your feet, and when they stop playing it's dinner time.

How big can a Lion get? When you run out of money feeding it, get a smaller Lion.

What are Lions good for? Terrorizing people and keeping people out of their land and making little Lions.

Is a Lion good for companionship? YES, as long as you can afford to feed them; if not you could be breakfast, lunch and dinner.

The Lion is the king of the jungle. Who is the Queen? The one he has the butt call with.

Do Lions get along with people? Only if they are not hungry.

Will Lions help people if they are in trouble? YES, they would eat them out of trouble.

In study one male Lion has all the female Lions in the pride, so he's got lot of freebies.

Does that means the male Lion is a pimp? No, he just gets a lot of butt calls.

Are all animals this way? NO, only Lions have a pride with a BIG DADDY.

Lions what all do they do? Sleep, kill, to eat; they sleep, kill to eat; then he makes baby lions, lots butt call.

Is it hard of the male Lion to take care of all those lady lions? No, the lady do the feeding; he just sleep and protect them and have a lot of Butt call.

Will Lions be around forever? YES, because no one will eat them.

Is the jungle only for the Lions? No, there are other animals there; thats why people don't get eaten much.

How did people learn about Lions? They studied them; one person is studying them and the other 20 people were watching his back.

So that means they are not safe? NO, they are very safe as long as you are miles, miles and miles away from them.

Cheetahs

What is a Cheetah?

It is a big kitty cat about the size of a dog called the Greyhound although it is fastest land animal in the world.

Is it good to have a cheetah as a pet? Yes, if you can stay alive with it.

Do they have friends? Yes, only if they're around when they are not hungry.

Can a Cheetah be around children? Only when they are little kittens; after they are grown up they could be lunch.

Is it ok to train a Cheetah? Yes, if you can do it very very fast.

Do Cheetahs eat a lot? Only when they are hungry. It could be an animal, or it could eat you out of house and home.

How can you tell a Cheetah is around? First all the animals start running. Then you see a lot of dust. A Cheetah just passed by you looking for lunch.

Can Cheetahs do things like all other animals? YES, and more. Just stay at least a mile in distance so you won't be dinner.

If a Cheetah sees you and you blink you could be lunch.

Will Cheetahs be good for other people to see? In a cage Yes, after they have been feed.

Can you look at them in the wild? YES, only if you are miles, miles, miles away and you are in a cage.

Will they just attack people? Yes and no, if they see you and they have eaten, you're safe, although if they see you and they are hungry, help can't help you. In fact help will need help to help you.

Out in the wild Cheetah run free, what would happen if you put one in a cage? It would run around in the cage until it falls apart, get out and eat the person that put it in the cage.

If a Cheetah was coming and I'm in the wild what can I do? First pray; second say, "Hello God."

Can a man outrun a Cheetah? YES, if he wants to live.

Is the wild safe life around Cheetahs? Yes, until lunch or dinner time.

Have the wild life ever had problem with Cheetahs? No, you can't talk to them so if you live with them you're lucky.

What's the best thing about the Cheetahs? They are fast and lunch is always close even if it is miles away.

Cheetah's the fastest animal in the world. It takes care of its own fast food and never losses a race.

Bears

What is a Bear?

It is a very big animal with a man's body shape with lots of fur over its body big claws and giant teeth and it growls all the time and eats everything – people if they are around.

Do Bears scare people? Only when you see one.

Can they kill you? YES, whenever they get ready and are hungry.

Is it safe to be around bears? Yes, when they're locked up and have been fed.

Do they ever hurt people? Only if you are around at dinner time.

What do bears eat? Only the things that don't eat them.

Where can you find a Bear? In the wilds if it's hungry it will find you.

What do you do if you see a Bear? Run as fast as hell before it sees you.

Will a Bear in the wild be safe for people? Only if they don't want to be the Bear's lunch.

Wild Bears is it hard to find them? If you are out in the wild they will find you; if they are hungry you could be dinner.

Has the wild life ever had problem with Bears? Only when it's time for Bears to eat, and if you are around you may have a problem.

How can you know when a bear is around? First the birds fly away; the trees start shaking, and you hear nothing but big claws hitting the ground and the ground start shaking; it's time to run.

The wild life is the Bear's world; what is there is his. If you want to visit don't stay long. You could camp out. If you go to sleep you could wake up as a Bear's breakfast.

Bears are one of the largest land animals in the world. If you see one, run before it sees you.

Bears love to eat; they don't mind the flavor; they just what to get full, so if you riding in your car and you see a bear and want to throw them a treat, don't do it. You could end up being the main course.

Bears basic walks on all fours all the time hunting in twenty miles areas looking for food. If you show, the bears will show out.

All Bears are alike. The biggest is the Grizzly Bear. If you know he's around, stay away, far, far away. They don't mind what they eat. JAWS don't mess with him.

A Grizzly stands 8 to 9 feet tall. That is not hard to see so when that bears get in sight, quickly turn around and run the other way. Your life will depend on it.

They have little bears called cubs. They are the size of a big dog, so if you ever see one don't try to play with it. If you can see the cub, the mother can see you. You could end up as the family meal.

Mountain Lions

What is a Mountain Lion?

It is a big cat that lives in the mountain.

How does a Mountain Lion look? It's a very big kitty cat with brown fur, long tail, and eats any type animals its gets its hands on.

Is it ok to pet a Mountain Lion? Yes, as long as it a baby. When it grows up, it can eat your hand for lunch.

Do people like Mountain Lions? YES, the one that don't live in the mountains.

What do you feed a Mountain Lion? As much as you can to keep them from eating you.

Do they make good pets? YES, when they're babies, but when they grow you could be their lunch.

Is it ok to see one in the wild? YES, but run before they see you.

How can you name one very easy? Call it anything just hope it never comes.

Are there a lot of them? YES, just don't go anywhere they are especially when they're hungry.

A Mountain Lion has all the area it wants to eat, so don't visit and stay too long. They are big cats, so don't end up an accidental lunch.

Will a Mountain Lion kill you? No, just eat you.

What are Mountain Lions? First it start out as a Little Kitten, then it turns in to a giant Kitty Cat and all they do is eat sleep, sleep eat, and then for more cats it makes a butt call, then make more kitty cats.

It's a big cat. When it show up, it shows out, so please stay away from its show so you won't be its desert.

A big cat with a big appetite, so stay away or you could be its lunch.

All cats like to eat. Mountain Lions like to crunch anything can be lunch.

Wild animals are always in the wild, so don't go where no man has gone before, because if you go you will be in the Mountain Lion back yard. That yard could be your last.

Meow meow kitty – they don't do that. They roar loud, so if you wanted to play with one, after it's over they have to be fed, so don't end up being dinner.

Are all big cats like Mountain Lions? No, they can live in the snow, can kill anything in the snow and eat it later and don't have to worry about a microwave.

Meow kitty kitty – big cats little cats, you should never go where they roam. They live alone; they never say hello just good bye.

If a Mountain Lion comes into your back yard, move out; they don't pay rent.

Elephants

What is an Elephant?

It is the biggest land animal on earth with a big nose.

Is it ok to play with an Elephant? Yes and no. They may not want to play with you.

Can they be safe to be around? Yes if you are miles away.

Do people like Elephants? Yes, until it's time to feed them.

Can an Elephant get big? YES, as long as they can eat they will grow, grow, grow, grow until you run out of money, you might be dinner.

Are Elephants hard to find? No, when they are around you will feel the earth quake.

Are they dangerous? Only when they see a mouse.

Are they easy to train? Yes, only if you say please first.

Do they make good pets? YES, only if you can buy a truck load with food for them every day.

The Elephant is the animal that goes where it wants, does whatever it wants to do they run in packs, it's their way or no way so stay out of their way.

They're too big to play with, so don't try to play with them. They will play with you if you can feed all of them.

They have a big nose. It's called the trunk, and they got a big butt, and they don't do butt calls.

They got big teeth. They call it the tusk. They can tear down trees, tear doors off cars, so if you see them go the other way.

Elephants live a very long time, so if you see a group of them, let them pass by, or you can get caught in a walk by.

The big, biggest is the giant that is the Elephant when you hear them, run, or you could be in their way, and you have a big, big problem.

Lion, Tigers and Bears are no match for the one and only Elephant. It's too big, too bad; that's how they roll.

It eats more than you in a life time. It eat that much in one week, and when it get a butt call, it's a double butt call.

Can people have an Elephant? YES; if you can feed it you can have one.

It eat as much as your pay check in one day; the next day you will have to dial 911 for back up.

Elephants are very smart. If they like you, you're ok, but check out before you feeding time.

Big Elephants, small Elephants, they will get big and when it happens they will show up and show out.

Rats

What is a Rat?

A small animal that will eat anything mostly in trash, hairy with whiskers and a long tail.

Can you play with them? YES, if your dumb and stupid.

Are they safe? YES, if you can find a clean one.

Do they like people? YES, if they are dirty and nasty.

Where can you find them? Anywhere you put something you don't want.

How do you get them out of your house? Buy a lot of cats.

Will we ever be safe around them? YES, if they're miles away.

Can you train one? YES, if you're that crazy and stupid.

Will rats ever have a place in the world? YES, if they go south and we go north.

Do they eat a lot? As long as there is trash they will be eating.

Can they do anything good? YES and NO. NO!

Have rats done anything to get in the news? YES, some have got so big that it was bigger than a dog.

Can they be of good use Only if you have trash that you don't need.

How old do they get? If they get old they been here too long.

Do mouse trap work? YES and NO, if they want cheese they would get a Big Mac.

Have kids ever had problems with rats? YES, if they were ever playing in trash.

They say that they hang around dumpsters where people throw their trash. YES, and them they don't pay rent, but they do get free Breakfast, lunch and dinner daily.

If you see an old house and you want to buy it and it's full of rats what do you do/ You do nothing; the rats own it.

Have the world got to where there are too many rats? That's how it always been, they have their side of the Town. It's called the dump; it's their side.

After all the things that are bad about them have they found anything that is good about them? YES, one. Nothing.

Rats will be here as long as we are, so if you see one, a thousand are looking at you.

Squirrels

What is a Squirrel?

It is a little animal that eats nuts, has a bushy tail that live in a tree. You will never see them go in their home.

A squirrel is so fast that if you drop food for them they would get it before it hits the ground and be back in their house.

They are so fast that if you put out 20 nuts they all will be gone by one squirrel before you get back in your house to see them do anything.

They are so fast that when they have sex they catch their lady friend and have a quickie in 2 seconds and make a lot of babies.

Squirrels can climb anything - poles, electric wires, and your house and see everything you do like in the bedroom.

They are very smart. They store their food for the winter, so if your food in your house disappeared you've been hit by the Squirrel bandit.

All squirrel are fast, so don't try to sneak up on one. It will be gone before you get there.

They are so quick, if you see one, think again. That was 10 of them; they all look the same.

All squirrels has a mate; they stay that way for life time until one get caught in a butt call.

They say some squirrel can go to the Olympics, only they're too fast for the time clock.

They say squirrels are so quick they don't even have

to work out because no trainer can keep up with them.

Lady and gentleman, they will try to film some squirrels in action. We put out some nuts. Sorry the camera was on, but it missed them all.

You can watch a squirrel in your yard. They will go up a tree into their nest but you can never see were they go in. People say they're too quick; some say they just disappear.

Never try to catch one; it will take a 100 people.

Never try to feed one; a thousand will show up.

Never try to watch them mate; one blink of your eye and you missed it all.

They have little squirrels; they grow to be quick as the big squirrels.

Squirrels look the same; if you see one you really so twenty.

Up and down the tree so fast, one goes up a different one come down. It happen so fast and it looked like the same one.

Never think you have just one squirrel in your yard. They also have families. That's why when you see one on the right, there are three on the left, and you never see them all at the same time.

You can try anything like spreading nuts around to see them. You will only see one. While you're watching him, the nuts are gone in all the other places.

All squirrels have fun tricking you. They use signal little sounds so when one comes out the rest have already been there.

Never think that if in family they have neighbors too.

Pigeons

What is a Pigeon?

It is a bird that flies around, little bigger than a baseball and it coos a lot. They hang around buildings and they crap on things a lot.

People feed them a lot. If they feed one, twenty will pop up so fast that it will scare you.

If you live close to town or in a high rise they make a lot of noises on window sills. Sleeping for people is impossible.

If you have a cat, and you see a lot of feathers on you porch, your cat just had lunch.

What is good about a pigeons? One they stay in groups where they get to eat.

How long have they been around? For years. They use to be homing pigeons to send messages until they stop coming back.

In New York it was so many, you came out of a building you see business people with umbrellas. You would think it was raining. NO they would tell you that the pigeons are flying by and they crap a lot.

Are they good for pets? Yes in a cage you take it out it will take a trip elsewhere.

Are they hard to catch? No just hard to keep.

If you have a pigeon and your neighbor has one, and you all don't know each other, and your pigeon gets away, then you see them with one, it could start a war.

People are always like to see them fly in groups. They fly so well together, although if they fly in your direction, run; they crap will be together too.

Do they get along with dogs? Some times until they crap on them.

In a lot of parks you have statues. Pigeons call it the Hollywood show. The statue are of famous people so it makes them famous too, so lights, camera, action – show time.

Can all people like pigeons? Yes if you like to get crapped on.

Are pigeons in the wild like the forest? No they like people to feed them, and crap on buildings.

What is good about pigeons? It's a pretty bird until you find out they crap a lot.

Why do they crap on things? They can't talk; it is the way they say thank you after you feed them.

Do pigeons get along with other birds? NO they want to be the only ones fed.

Do other birds like pigeons? NO because if the pigeons were not here, they would be getting fed by the people instead of them.

Is it safe to be around pigeons? YES until someone scares them and they fly away and you don't get crapped on.

Do they do anything other they crapping? YES they eat, then fly, then crap.

Can't that crapping be called something other than crap? YES, it is DO-DO. OK?

How can you get rid of pigeons? Easy get some cats. They will be gone quickly, but you will have a lot of meowing meowing.

I like pigeons. They take you where no one has gone before – not outer space but give you a lot of crap.

Eagles

What is an Eagle?

It is the biggest bird in America and it's our Nation symbol, and if it's hungry, it will eat anything around. It will eat your chickens, your cat, your rabbit if you have one.

It has claws so big that if your dog comes up missing, it was the Eagle's lunch.

So out in the wild if you go fishing, and you get a big fish on your line, and the Eagle hungry, you will only get half.

Eagle nests are very big about the size of a good coffee table, big enough to hold food for three, Mama, Daddy and the big baby.

It is by law illegal to kill an Eagle, so they can go anywhere. If they're in your tree they're OK; if they're on your porch they're OK; if they're at your party they're looking for a butt call.

All Eagles are very powerful strong, so if you let your puppy out to play, do it after they have had lunch so the little puppy will not be the Eagle's lunch.

As an American we're proud to have that bird as our symbol. It does a lot of shows at football games. It will fly in from top of the stadium to the center of the field to land on the arm of the trainer and carry them of if it's hungry.

What is good about Eagles? It has a white head and red on its back, and it don't crap on people.

What do Eagles like to eat? Anything they can pick up from the ground or in water with their claws for breakfast, lunch or dinner.

Do Eagles have rights? YES the right that people don't have.

The Eagles can live with the easy life, fly high in the sky but stay low from a 747 airplane.

Do Eagles have a legal fly zone? YES up and down.

Will Eagles laws ever change? YES if they move to another country.

What made them so special the Government? Who voted them in to be the symbol of America? Congress at a happy hour.

If the Eagles ever become extinct, what will take its place? It would be the America the pigeon; it's everywhere?

They say that Eagles can see almost a mile away to find food. What happens when they get old and can't see far? They will use Amazon internet services for home delivery.

If I was an Eagle I would fly to a place so I could be King and get a lot of butt calls.

Eagles will mate for life, so they don't know about marriage or divorces.

Eagles always fly over water and catch fish right out of it barely touching the water. Is the Eagle smart or are the fish dumb?

Eagles can catch rabbits because they're never looking up and it is too late when they're looking down when the Eagles are flying in the sky. They become the Eagle's lunch.

The Eagle is the big bird that eats a lot, flies a lot, and don't crap on people just on flying airplanes.

Giraffes

What is a Giraffe?

It is an animal that has a super long neck, long legs looks like a super-giant Ostrich; the Giraffe is a mammal not a bird.

This animal has no problem with food; they eat from tops of trees where no man has gone before.

This animal is so tall it can walk by your second story window in your house and watch you when you get a butt call.

This animal is so tall it can watch movies at a drive in theater without buying a ticket.

This animal is so tall it can slam dunk without having to jump.

This animal can block a shot in basketball with its horns.

If basketball was played on grass, giraffes would have an animal sport.

If you had a lot of Giraffes together it would look like a mountain was moving.

All Giraffes have a very long neck. If you see one full grow with neck of three feet, that is called a midget Giraffe.

Giraffes have only one friend, the monkeys because in trees they see things eye to eye.

The Giraffes has long legs and they are very strong; they use them for protection. If football ever need a kicker, I vote for the Giraffes.

If you ever go to a concert outside like Woodstock take a giraffe. They can tell you everything that is going on in the show and they don't need a ticket.

I vote Giraffe see all, know all.

The Giraffe is the tallest animal in the world; only problem is if it drops something, it's down the drain.

If there was the last apple in the world, and the Giraffe had to eat it to stay alive, and the wind blow it off the tree, and it hit the ground, it would have a problem.

All giraffe have long legs. They can run very fast although they have problem stopping. Their legs stop; the necks keep going.

The Giraffes are in most zoos; some are nice and you can feed the when they're young. Don't give them something they don't like; they will give it back. They have a long tongue.

Everything on Giraffes are long. When they mate the males have no problem; they have very long tools that makes connection to female like a butt call.

People ride through areas where they have wild animals. It is hot all the time. They open their sun roof for air, the giraffes will put their head in to get some air to.

Giraffes have one problem with water, when it's time to drink they have to get down to the water by spreading it's legs apart to get closer to the ground to get the water. They have to get low, low, low.

Giraffes has it highs and lows. The only other animals that eat like them is the Elephant. It has trunk it can reach up and down, so how to get food, first come first served.

Do Giraffes get along with people? YES, they have long neck, and long legs; they like tall people.

I think Giraffes will be around a long time. If you need a tree trimmed, call a Giraffe.

Hyenas (The Laughing Hyena)

What is a Hyena (laughing Hyena)?

It is an animal that is from Africa. It has great thing about it as a dog. It's not like the dogs here in America. It don't bark it LAUGHS.

They run in packs like wolfs, in large groups twenty or more, growling and laughing.

If they're hungry, they Laugh.

If they want to mate, their females laugh.

If their pack wanted to attack an animal to eat, they all do a lot of laughing.

When they're mating, the male will throw up his nose and do a lot, a lot, of laughing.

When new puppies are born in to the pack, the pack has a Laughing party.

The laughing is the sound that all the animals know about. When they hear the laughing they run the other way, although the trap is to trap their pray. They run into a pack who is quite, then they laugh at dinner time.

The laughing is their communication: one laugh call, two laughs problem, three laughs get the hell out. We have a problem.

Why don't they bark like dogs, they look like dogs? They laugh because they are African dogs.

Africans call them the laughing hyena for a long time. Well the hyena is name, and the sound they make is like laughter and they look funny. Their head is higher and their butt is low; that looks funny too.

This is a funny animal. They laugh at everything. When they are a wake they laugh; instead of snoring in their sleep, they laugh in their sleep.

If the chase something to eat, and it get away, they laugh but they're still hungry.

As the day is over and the sun is going down, they don't just go to sleep, they laugh their self to sleep.

I think that it's a great thing for them to have a special way of communicating, their laughter. We always hear them laughing.

I think that laughing is good. That means you're happy, but they're not happy but when they're hungry they are still laughing.

Laughing hyena is very spiritual. The Pigmy's look up to the laughing hyena because they're not laughing because they're short.

Wolves run in packs, Lions run in prides, the laughing hyenas run in packs, and I think they like it because they're always laughing.

In Africa some people say the laughing hyenas are ZULU. That means bad spirit, because when it is thundering and lightning and raining hard, they're running around laughing.

If you can laugh at anything people say you're crazy, although they laugh and it's not a damn thing, they are still crazy.

The history of the laughing hyena has never been solved, and they ask the laughing hyena why you are always laughing? They said because in Africa there is nothing else to do.

7. Professional Job Occupations

Attorney	124
Doctor	127
Witch Doctor	130
Policeman	133
Fireman	137
Bus Driver	139
Truck Driver	142
Airplane Pilot	145
Cruise Captain	148
News Report	150
Window Washer	152
Taxi Driver	156
Astronaut	159
Story	161
Forest Ranger	163
Singer	167
Actor	170
Movie Star	173
Stunt Man	176
Comedian	180

The Attorney

What is an Attorney?

This is a person that you hire for law problems, to sue for something, to represent you in court, or to represent your business or when someone is trying to sue you.

Mr. Attorney, can you help me? Help you in what? If I go to court they say since I didn't go last time they're going to lock me up this time. So can you tell them to let me have the last time back?

Mr. Attorney, can you help me if I commit a crime? What crime? I have not did it yet, I just wanted to know if you could get me out of the crime I commit? What crime is that? I don't know yet.

Mr. Attorney, can you sue her for me? Sue her for what? Because I like her but she don't like me? Is that what she said? No I haven't asked her yet.

Uncle Attorney is someone who sues people., Can you help to sue them first? Why someone would want to sue you? Because on the internet they said if someone is going to sue you, so I want to sue them first.

Mr. Attorney, can you get me out of Jail? They said I committed a crime. Did you do the crime? NO, I was driving down the street my friend asked me for a ride. I was dropping him off at his house; the police pull up, pull their gun on us and said get out of the car with your hands up. So that what we did. They looked in his bag it was full of money. I'm locked up; can you get me out?

YES and NO, Yes you have a case; I think this is one is for PERRY MASON.

There is now a problem. She said I did it and I did not do it. It was because about her. I thought about doing it, after I thought on it more, can't do it. Even if she paid me I'm not able to do it. The Attorney said what is it she wants you to do? Get married I just wanted a Butt Call.

Mr. Attorney is your client here today? NO. Why is he not here? Because he was not at the place where the crime was committed? We have on tape and it's no mistake that it was him. The Attorney stepped up to plead his case in court and bring this case to a conclusion. We have here two Identical twins brothers. One is here committing a crime the other one who is accused is not him because when the crime was being committed he was in the bed with the Judge's daughter That is why he is not here today.

Mr. Attorney, can you keep me out of Jail? I don't know what you did. I saw a crime and they said I don't come and tell them what happen I'll go to Jail. Well tell me what happen. He went in McConnell and took some money and got away. They said I have been paid and they told me what to say. It was a drive by, and it was not. It was a walk by. He just ran out with the money and got away.

Uncle Attorney, I need some money. Can I sue some people and get it? What people do you want to sue? The people at the Bank on the corner. Can't we do it? They got too much money. Can't we just get a little of it? You just can't just sue them; you have to have a reason. OK if I asked for some money and they did not give it to me. Would that be a reason to sue them? NO. How much do you need? I will give it to you, NO that's OK. If you give it to me, then you could sue me and get it back.

The Doctor

What is a Doctor?

He or she are people that you go to when you sick to get help and get well and when you get well, you get a bill. The cost of the bill make you sick again.

Doctor, I need some help. I'm in love with the beautiful woman. What can I do to make her fall in love with me? Does she know you? NO. Have you talked to her? NO. Has she even seen you? NO. If you love her I would stop right there while you're in control.

Mr. Doctor, all of my friends are so pretty, have great figures, plus good stylish hair. Why come you don't have all of those beautiful things too? Because every time I start on me, all of them need something. So your their stylist for their good looks? YES. So you need some new friends.

Mr. Doctor, I need a new heart. What's wrong with this one? It's broken again. He left me for another woman. Why? I don't know; I loved him to death. That why he left; he thought you was going to kill him with sex.

Mrs. Doctor, Can you change my looks so women would love me more? I give it a try. A year later, Doctor, can you make me like I was? What's wrong? Five women want me; four already have me; seven want to kill me because of what all the other women are doing with me. Doctor, Doctor, what are you doing? Oh now, not you too.

Mrs. Doctor, I can't sleep for days. I work hard; I even work out; I just can't sleep. What could I do? Tonight get your favorite food, get your favorite movie and you and your husband have sex and call me the next day. The next day, ring, ring. Hello how did it go? You get some sleep? YES, that great, but Doctor. But what? The lady said, now I'm pregnant.

Uncle Doctor can you give me a note to stay at home from school? Are you sick? No. Why do you want to stay at home from school? Someone is going to beat me up. Everyone is laughing; she made me hold her hand, and tomorrow I have to do it again, and if I don't she going to beat me up. I tell you try this. I think she'll leave you alone. OK. He how did it go? I did like you said; I tried to KISS her and she ran away. Thanks Uncle.

Mr. Doctor, can you help me? My whole life is over. What is your problem? My girlfriend she wants to get married have children, and I didn't know if I ready for all that. This is what you do; tell her for the children let's get started. We'll have sex three time a night then we will have children; after that we'll get married. Hey Doctor I will be off the hook. What happened after first two nights? She said she change her mind. Things are fine the way they are. That Viagra works.

Mrs. Doctor, how are you today? What is wrong today? Well nothing. You're such a beautiful woman I think I fallen in love with you. Well son I'm your Doctor. But I love you. Well OK come over to my house for dinner tomorrow. Sure great, ring, ring. Come on in. Have a look around. Come follow me OK. Hey this is a bedroom. Come lets have sex, sex, and more sex said the Doctor.,Come back young man. He ran, then the door slam. The young man was gone. Then the Doctor said, I'm a Doctor it works every time with a patient.

Mr. Doctor, what is the problem? I want girls to like me. Now do this: get too Big Mac's, a grape crush drink and some Bar-B-Q Lays potatoes chips. Before you eat them you have to spin to the left ten times; then eat your meal and spin back the right way ten times. Then go to sleep and the next day tell me what happen. Next day ring, ring. Help, help, how do you make it stop? The girls everywhere they just won't leave me alone. Enjoy it; the magic it only last 48 hours.

The Witch Doctor

What is a Witch Doctor?

They are historically doctors before time, before we had electricity, before cars, indoor plumbing. The Africans Doctors, Indian Doctors, and Tribal Doctors they got the medicine from Mother Nature.

Mr. Witch Doctor, I have a head ache. What can you do to help me? Find a cold spring, stick your head in it, and come see me when it get well. Then I will know if it works.

Mr. Witch Doctor, a lot of people have colds. What can we do? Start a big fire, put them around it It will warm them up.

Mr. Witch Doctor, a lot of people has the whooping cough. Help us. Go to the basketball court and shoot hoops for a few hours. Call me and tell me if that makes it go away.

Mr. Witch Doctor, my girlfriend doesn't love me anymore. How do you know? She told me so. Then call her on the phone, call her by another name and tell me what happened. Next day. What happened? I was wrong; she still loves me. She meant she did not love her other boyfriend.

Mrs. Witch Doctor, my husband said I'm not the same woman he married. Doctor, What did he say was wrong? I don't look as good as I used to; I'm not as sexy as I used to be. What can I do? Ask him when you get home does he what you to go back to your old boyfriend. Ring, ring. Hello Doctor. YES, I did what you said. What happened? He fell down and said please stay, please stay. You look better than my old girl friend.

Mr. Witch Doctor, why do girls like girls and men like men? That's a good question. But when animals start doing it we have a big problem.

Mr. Witch Doctor, my husband wants a boy so bad. We have three girls. What can we do? First you and your husband on the next full moon, get two big Mac's, two grape crush drinks, a big bag of Lays Bar-b-q potatoes ships, spin around together ten time to the left then eat your meal, then make love two time and then spin around to the right ten times. A year later they called the Doctor and said thank you. Then the Doctor said what happened? I got pregnant. We had triplets - three boys. Thank you so much.

Mr. Witch Doctor, my team is trying so hard to win some basketball games. Can you help us? OK from now on at practice have your team to practice dribbling basketballs backward and then for the rest of the season just do that. Five games later they called the Doctor. Thank you Doctor we are winning now. The Doc said it works every time.

Mr. Witch Doctor, can I ever get a girlfriend? YES, now next girl you meet ask her will you be my girlfriend if I leave my other girlfriend. Just try it and let me know. Three days later, ring, ring. How did it go. Great, until the girl I liked were all sisters so I like them all. It was three of them; they were triplets.

Mr. Witch Doctor, can you help me? I want to be a move star. What kind of a star and actor? Here is what you do. Get a Webster's Dictionary; read all of it, then move to Hollywood. Go to Paramount Studios tell them the Witch Doctor sent you. A STAR IS BORN.

The Policeman

What is a Policeman?

He or she is the person to protect the people from the bad people that commit illegal crimes, break the law. They get a company car and free gas, some even free rent.

Mr. Policeman, can you help me? Someone stole my car, can you help me get to work? Well I'm on duty I can't take you but I can give you bus fare. OK. Get on the bus. Good morning everyone, it happen again. It work. This is the free bus fare again.

Mr. Policeman, help. A man stole my purse from me and it had my rent money in it. What am I going to do? Where am I going to live, me and my kids out in the streets? Well let me make a report and there are people that can help you with your rent. Thank you, you're such a nice man. Hour later, stop that bus. Lady this ain't no city bus. We're going to Los Vegas. I know I got money now. They going to pay my rent.

Mrs. Police lady, someone stole my bicycle. It was the newest model, the 1000 ROAD STAR. My mother is going to kill me. My daddy is going to kill me; brother is going to beat me up because it was his bicycle. I was just going to the store. I will make a report and it might show up. Well now you go home. No can't go home. Can't I go with you because they're going to kill me.

Mr. Policeman, one day I was riding in my area. This beautiful lady comes out to her mail box. Then the wind blow and open her robe. She had big everything - big butt, big tits. I said need some help? She said yes if you help me make some coffee. I said OK and she said OK. I said this sound like a butt call.

Mr. Policeman, this pretty lady stopped a policeman and said I lock my keys in my car. Can you help me get them out? He pulls out his slim Jim. Click, click, you can get in it's open. She got in her car and left. Then a man showed up and said, Is there a Jaguar around here? The Policeman said it just left with a fine lady in it. I need that butt call.

Two Policemen him and his partner. Driver says how's your wife? She's crazy; she's complains about my job. Well go home and ask this, You want me to go back to my ex-wife? OK next day, Good morning, Joe. Hey it worked. What happened? Did what you said, I get two butt calls every night.

Mrs. Police lady said good morning to Mike her partner. Mike said how is it going with your husband? He's complaining again. He said this job is not safe for a woman. Look Jackie, you're a Police lady, Woman of the Month twice in five months. You've made history. Mike is your vacation time coming up? Yes. Well OK. Next day, thanks Mike. I did what you said. I told him in my own way, if he stop complaining and let me do my job, on the vacation you can have as many butt calls that you want. I've got the power now.

Mr. Policeman, I am a detective on stake-out for drug deal tonight at this address. Car pulls up three people pull out two big suits. Ten minutes later two more cars pull up five people, two more suites. We wait; everyone ready; we make the move, front door, back door 1,2,3, kick in the door. They said surprise! Happy birthday party although they was at the wrong house.

Mrs. Police lady, I was walking a beat in River Gate Mall, Madison, Tennessee. A little boy was crying. What a wrong little boy? He said I want my daddy. A man run over. I said to him, Are you his daddy? He said yes. He told his little boy, we are going to McDonald's later. The little boy said, Can we go with the Pretty Police lady? Two months later the Police lady and that man got married.

The Fireman

What is a fireman?

Men or women working to protect people from fire problem houses, apartment, cars and the forest fire. That's Smokey the Bear department. He needs help all time. The firemen are on their job even on a Butt calls.

Firemen sitting around; call comes in; cat up a tree, one unit heads out to the address, a house call big dog at the bottom of the tree. Get rid of the big dog; cat come down the tree by itself. On the way back to the firehouse another call. Car fire on Main street two blocks away. We get there. There's a 85 Mustang on fire in a parking lot; we put out the car fire. A bank alarm goes off. Bank robbery, bank robbers run to the Mustang. No one gets away. The bank robber's car it was the one on fire. BUSY DAY.

Mr. Fireman visits class career day. Mr. Fireman, are fires super big? NO sometimes we have little ones. Mr. Fireman, if a lady jumps out of a window can you catch her? YES and NO if it's a little lady and she follow directions, everything can be OK. But Mr. Fireman, what if she's super big lady can you do anything to help the people? We have something for her. It's a big net that we can hold out for her and ask God to help us.

Mrs. Fire lady class room visit career day. Miss Fire lady, what do you do when a fire happens? I do everything to put out the fire and get people to safety. What is that? Put the hose and the water on the hottest part of the fire. What is that, it is where the fire started? What is that? We can't tell that until we put the fire out. Next question. Not you, someone else.

Mr. Fireman in Long Beach in California early morning call, morning fire at a car dealership 1313 Pacific Coast High way Boulevard at Colletto Nissan Car Dealership. We get there; the fire is in a car. We get started and get the other cars out of the line of the fire, get the fire under control only two cars burnt. Talked to the owner, a beautiful lady. We had coffee, talked about better fire protection. Two month later we got married.

Mr. Fireman long day, night call comes in emergency child problem. House two blocks away lady answers the door of the house. We ask her what the problem is, children running around scramming and laughing. Then she said come to the bedroom. The little boy had his head caught in the head board of a brass bed. We said it was a little problem we'll have him out in a few minutes. We told the little boy we can help you. Everyone is laughing at me the little boy said. I said we can get you out. You can put on my fireman hat, and we'll let you blow the siren on the fire truck, and we will even ride you around the block. The two firemen pulled on the brass and the little guy was right out. He got the fireman's hat, blew the horn on the fire truck and road around the block. After that the little guy said I want to be a fireman when I grow up.

Ms. Fire Lady early morning Nashville, Tennessee, 7:30 am a call came in from TWA Truck stop with 18 wheelers on the lot. This area had drug dealers, fast ladies call girls 24 hour service for butt calls. Location four blocks away on a route crossing main street bridge looking down at the fire making plans. Three fire units are heading in; they are moving the 18 wheelers out of the fire area. We got two trailers burning with AutoZone products in one; the second was a flat bed with wood products on its back, and it's on fire. We got the hoses on the fire; 45 minutes everything was under control. The fires was out; we doubled checked for hot spots. The TV cameras, the helicopters cameras were on site. The fire fighters we done. Owner job. Everything was back to normal. We pulled out those 18 wheelers so fast in record breaking time. The TWA is back open for business. There was some girls saying we can give you firemen discounts on butt calls.

The Bus Driver

What is a Bus Driver?

Men and women drive buses local, long distance. Buses are very important to get people to work and to go out of town and take long trips. A lot of people like to go to the Casino to gamble and get butt call.

Mr. Bus driver, you been driving buses for 25 years. What is the one thing you wish you did not have to deal with? Those loud bad kids. The deal is they all have been put out of regular school and go to the school for bad kids. I go by there, and there's one is so bad he just have to go there. They don't have class for him because he's so bad.

Mr. Bus Driver, what is the worst thing that you have had to go through, in your time here? People complaining about the air conditioning. One will say it too cold then one will say it's too hot; back and forth they got to fighting about it. It scared me to death. Some man on the bus stop them from fighting and the people on the bus did not mind. Those women had some big everything - big tits, big butts. They had to get a whole of something to just get them two apart. Those men on the bus said it was almost like a butt call video.

Mr. Bus driver, it was early in the morning about 7:30 a.m. a group of people on their way to gamble in Los Vegas. The bus was loaded. This one black lady 36-24-38, her back yard was on fire. We talked all the way there then we go off and got married. We been together for twenty years. Got five kids and one more on the way. We're very happily married. I get all the butt calls I want from my wife – problem solved.

Ms. Bus driver, late one night stopping in Dallas Texas, I was driving a Greyhound with people on the bus. Some people meet on my bus. Everyone got on, we took off on the 45 freeway west bound. Two hours later a man came up to me and said I think we have a problem. There is a woman in the bathroom with a man and she is screaming. That's OK. They do that every week to get away from their husband and wife. It's an affair thing. They just like it on the bus thing.

Mr. Bus driver, I was on my way to Atlantic City. Everyone was sleep. They was a gambling group on there to a gambling convention. We got there; everyone checked in. One lady, very beautiful, came up to me and said you are a great driver. Is there anything we can do for you? Well most of the time when I get back they just pass the hat, and they give me a nice tip. Will you come with me so I can give you my tip? Now it was an all-day, all night butt call, because she came, but she did not gamble – problem solved.

Mr. Bus driver, it was colder than the South Pole that day. I was in Alaska. Snow was about five feet deep, and the plows had cleared the road after a heavy snow. I was in a Brand new Greyhound Bus. The snow was to heavy unlimited levels today. We made it to Fairbanks. Everyone got off. I went and checked the bus. Someone left a carry-on bag full of money. I looked outside. I was not to leave for ten hours, so I thought that they would be back to get it. The money was in hundreds; it was just me and the mechanic, so I went back to the bus and counted the money 500,000 dollars.

Ten hours was over the people started to board the bus. On the way back I called my wife told her. She said what you going to do? It happen on the job? I'll just turn it in. She said how much is it? Told her I counted it and it was 500, 000 dollars. What? You better get some of that. You know we need a new car; the one we got is always breaking down, and the kids never stop needing stuff. But you be careful with it you never know.

I got back in and told them the story. So they will hold on to it to see if someone calls about it. How long? Two mouths. Went home to my wife and gave her 30,000 thousand. They wouldn't know. She's been my wife all these years; she deserve some of the luck that has come in my life. I told her that she could only spend a little at a time. Well the two mouths was over. They gave me the money. I put money away for my kids college fund, gave 20,000 thousand to my job health fund. Put some money in church. After all of that it was only 80,000 left. The rest I put in the bank for rainy days. Never made that bus trip again but one time me and my wife and the kids rented a van on a summer weekend. We drove up to Fairbanks to see the bus stop where I found the money. When I was driving off it was a very strange looking Eskimo he waved at us and had on a big smile and kinda laughing and look at us until we could not see him anymore.

The Truck Driver

What is a Truck Driver?

Men and women that drive trucks for transporting food products; they transport cars for sale; shows for concerts; special shipment for government, and most of all to move people from home to home.

Mr. Truck driver, what up out there? You have breaker, breaker, on? Have your CD on channel 19 you got EZE. I'm rolling down the 45 freeway east bound. Is there any smokies out there? What up EZE? You got King Lincoln on the 19 channel. The smokies are creeping around and around. They hop off and on the down low. You can roll right on in to Cashville. If you early at the TWA you might catch a Butt Call. Breaker, Breaker this is EZE. I got you on that talk, talk. King Lincoln if they're down there you got a cold one on me. EZE out. Got to keep my eye on the freeway I'm rolling on.

Ms. Hot Pants, I got you on the 19 fired up on this 65 north bound rolling through this Cool Springs ready to camp down in Cashville. What up Hot Pants? You got EZE on your line. This is Hot Pants. What you need Miss Hot Pants? You got Hot Pants. I need some fun, a good time and a twelve-pack. Miss Hot Pants, I got all that. I don't do twelve-packs. I do cases and they already Ice cold. Meet me at the TWA in Cashville. You can set me on fire. I will EZE;,you talking my talk. All right I'll see you in a short short. This is Hot Pants, EZE. I got my ears on for you; I'm going through Bellevue on 45 East bound. See you in a short short. EZE breaker breaker on you, Hot Pants.

What up out there? You got EZE about to pull in here in Cashville at the TWA. What up Miss Hot Pants? You got your ears on? What up EZE? This is your Hot Pants. I got you loud and clear. This is EZE ready to pop the tops off a cool one for you Miss Hot Pants baby. You talk real nasty; what is on your mind, Mr. EZE? Come on and meet me in the lobby of the TWA, Miss Hot Pants. EZE just wants to make you happy, Miss Hot Pants. OK Mr. EZE. Let's get this party started alright. Alright see you in a short short.

Mr. Truck driver, for all you truckers you got EZE on the 19 breaker, breaker. It Friday Night here in Nashville. We going to have a little party at Billy Joe's, at the corner, of 5th and main. You all are welcome to come. Just put your truck at the TWA. It just two blocks east of the TWA. Now if the fast girls pop up they like to have fun too. If you need help, just get on the hot box. Everybody knows Billy Joe's. See you there in a short short.

Mr. Truck driver, this is EZE on the hot box. We are right here at Billy Joe's. The party is popping and the girls are hot; the beer is ICE cold. Billy got the hot wings hopping. YES Sir, Billy Joe's DJ is jam to Jam Jamming. In his party spot if you need help just fire up your breaker, breaker. Will be right on you. This is EZE. See you in a short short.

Mr. Truck driver, this is EZE on the hot box channel 19. If you didn't make the big party at Billy Joe's last night it was so hot, we going light it up again. Saturday night it will start at 5:00 p.m. until you all have had enough, so hit the hot spot tonight. Get your girlfriends or your boyfriend. You can even bring your butt call. It's all going to be popping. This is EZE on the hot box. Check you in a short short. Breaker, breaker on channel 19, you got King Lincoln on the hot box. I was there last night and I'm still on fire. I'll be there again at Billy Joe's doing the DO. Billy Joe's got it and I want some more of it. This is King Lincoln. See you in a short short.

Mr. Truck driver, Breaker, breaker, channel 19. This is Hot pants. This is for Billy Joe. Your spot is hot baby. The hot wings will set you on fire. I was there last night. I got to have some more and that beer was ICE cold. It was cold as a ICEBERG. I'm going to get me some more of that fun. This is Hot Pants. See you at Billy Joe's tonight. See you in a short short. Hot Pants still on fire.

The Airplane Pilot

What is an Airplane Pilot?

Men and women that fly an air craft commercial and domestic. They have to take it up and carefully make it land safely.

Mr. Airplane Pilot, it was a beautiful day I was flying a private jet. I was flying over the Bermuda Triangle. I saw five flashing lights. They were flying one behind the other and they stopped in mid air on my left. I passed them. They were about a hundred yards away. I passed them. I call it in to the space station. They said YES we saw them and they disappeared. I said OK I didn't think I was crazy. Hey you guys they're back on my right side. The station, No Bill, we don't have nothing on the radar screen but you. But I see them, the same five. They little, flying around with each other in a circle and even up and down right beside my plane on my right-side. All we see is you and that fancy jet you be flying for Eric the Cunningham. But what the hell? They're right almost in my window. There go a lot of red lights. They're as big as a Hummer just doing as they please in the air right in front of me. What the hell? They just flew up through the clouds. They're gone now. Ah Bill, just tell us about it when you get back.

Ms. Airplane Pilot, I was flying out of Nashville for a group going to Atlanta to a Braves Game. Everyone got on the airplane. We took off smooth as silk and then on my right it look like a big round ball with light going around and around. It was flashing red and yellow; it was flashing silver. My copilot saw it, but he pass out. It was like sitting beside the left side of the plane. The stewardess came up and said the people are freaking out. It was big as a five bedroom house. It just sat beside us, and then the light got brighter off and on off and on like it was taking a picture. I tried to call it in and it was gone. The people on the plane was doing everything, laughing, screaming, crying. I talk to the station in Atlanta something was on the screen. Nashville said the same thing but it was there for only ten minutes.

Mr. Airplane Pilot, this was the story that I could not believe it really happen. Still can't believe it today. Me and my brother we entered the plane in Los Angeles, California, at the LAX flying to a Raiders and Cowboy game in Dallas Texas. We left at 9:00 Saturday morning having fun; a few friends seeing us off. We took off, talked and laughed. We had a few beers. We were in the air about two hours. Then flashing lights went off and on. Then it was like we were out in snow, dark black and just cold. It was wet and sticky hands all over our bodies. It went on and on flashing lights, darkness, hot, cold like a micro wave. I tried to call my brother but things and other things were in my mouth. I was so scarred I peed on myself and the wetness like my pee just vanished. I was thinking what is going on? I was crying, couldn't see anything, and it went on for hours. Then I passed out, then woke up in LAX 10:15. I hit my brother and woke him. What the hell is going on? We left LAX 9:00 am Saturday and it's 10:30 like we never left. What happened for the HOUR and a HALF hour?

Things Happen.

What plane takes off get in the air start flying around in a circle like a spinning top? A plane trying to be a Helicopter.

What plane takes off flies a long way then lands in water? A plane trying to a boat.

If you get on a plane it's taking off, and they want you to get off but won't give you a parachute, what do you do? That's a good question.

The Cruise Ship Captain

What is a Cruise Ship Captain?

A person that has the authority to command a ship that travels on water. Also to keep a look out for JAWS, and icebergs.

What happens when the ship start to sink? What should the Captain say? I have to go down with my ship? These days they call a helicopter to pick them up.

If your ship is about to run into another ship what do you do? They go to the right and you go to your right. No more problems or call Bruce Leroy.

If a ship is sinking and you can help what would you do? Send them some crazy glue and tow them in to the dock.

If you were on a cruise ship and you was leaving a party and saw someone fall over board what would you do? Scream "over board" back up the ship; throw a life preserver; pull them back a board. If it's a woman, she would owe you a butt call – problem solved.

If this was a cruise ship and they say they saw JAWS, what would you do? I would tell them we need a bigger boat. And call the Navy to blow his ass up.

If you were on a cruise ship and all the women where single what would you do? I would tell them I just won the Powerball. I get paid when we get back. I need a few butt calls, ASAP.

After you heard so many ships have had a lot of problems at sea, and you were on board at sea, what would you do? I would say I am very sick and need to go ashore now.

If you meet a beautiful lady and she asked you to go on a trip on a ship for a cruise and it was leaving tomorrow would you go? Only if I could look at her private to make sure she was a women and that I could get some good butt calls – problem solved.

If you were on a ship taking a Cruise and the ship started to sink and you had one wish what would you wish for? I was at home with 10,000,000 dollars tax free. With that I could get as many butt calls as I wanted.

If you entered a contest to win a cruise for a week and you won and you could take any woman in the world, who would it be? PAM GRIER as brown sugar – problem solved.

If you and your girlfriend was going on a cruise trip and the Captain said all aboard, and she was not there, would you leave her or wait for her? If I'm paying for it I would leave. It's my money. If she was paying for it, I would wait. If it was my money I would find a new girlfriend on the trip. But I would tell my girlfriend at home I was thinking of her every second when I get back.

You are out on a cruise ship. All the women keep looking at you. What would you do? Say can we meet in your room and talk and give them the business. You find out a lot of things behind closed doors. But if they were all transvestites, I would jump that ship.

What if you were on a ship and it started to sink and they were out of life boats and JAWS invited all his family? I would pray to God and ask if I could be like JESUS and walk the water and get the hell out of there – problem solved.

The News Reporter

What is a News Reporter?

It is a person that goes out in the public and different location and report the news of what happens like sports, things in school, business, good things and bad things and who hit the power ball.

Ladies and gentleman we are on the main street bridge in Nashville, Tennessee. There's a man here said he is going to jump if his wife leaves him. He has been standing up there for two hours. We have his wife here. Why is your husband doing this? I did not say I was going to leave him. I told him I was going to put him out if he doesn't get a job. He has to take care of his kids too. Mr. Mack did you hear what she said? Oh I said she was going to leave me with those kids and they could kill me. I don't have to work. The people pay me to keep them at home because they are so bad.

Ms. Cunningham all the years you been reporting news, what has been your best story? It was a bank robbery with people being held hostage with two men inside with machine guns, in military bullet proof outfits on, masks and everything. All of a sudden the doors opened. Money was flying everywhere. People was running out to get the money. The men ran out and threw the money everywhere, thousands and thousands of dollars. The police could not stop the people in the way of the men who were robbing the bank. The men got away with still bags full of money. As they were getting away they was still throwing money away to the people. The police never got a chance to catch the men? I call the people that got in the away the lucky ones because they needed the money and they never had to give it back.

Hello I'm here at North High School in Nashville, Tennessee. We are here for the finals of the Nation Spelling Bee. I'm here with the winner Charles Frost. How did you do it Charles? Every day I would read words and spell them from the World Book Encyclopedia. Well that was great, Charles, and it paid off. You got your trophy. If there was anything else you could have what would it be? A Big Mac every day for the rest of my life. Well there you have it right here at North High in Nashville, Tennessee. Aletha Cunningham over and out. Hey let's get Charles some Big Macs.

Dennise Cunningham on sight reporting right here in Nashville, Tennessee. The Titian just had a miracle play to advance to the Super Bowl to play St. Louise Rams. This is history in the making. It going on the record book. The Titians' next game will be in the Super Bowl. The city is light up. It will never be the same This is Dennise Cunningham in Nashville, Tennessee. The Super Bowl. Look out The Nashville Titians are on their way. This is Dennise Cunningham. I'm out. They going to have an after party. I have to report that too. We're out. Go Titians.

Why do you report on the same story more than the other ones? So the people can hear it twice. No really they did the story wrong the first time.

Why do you report a story? To let the people know; to report the story so everyone can hear the news.

Why do you report on a story more than once? To do it better the second time? No because they did the wrong story the first time.

Is a story a story or is it stories? No a story is the news.

After a story has been reported is the story over? No they do it again because some people may not have seen it.

If I report a story on you, will you report a story on me? No because I don't even know you.

Are all stories good to report? YES Are the bad stories good to report? YES to the bad people.

So rich stories are good for the rich people, the poor stories are for the poor people? No the rich stories are good for the poor people, to show them how not to be poor.

The Window Washer

What is a Window Washer?

It is a person that washes windows on the streets, on big buildings and sky scrapers. Some hang on ropes on the buildings. They even can see what people are doing inside.

Mr. Window Washer, tell me some of the things you have seen washing windows in the big buildings. A woman was having sex with her male boss. The woman boss was having sex with her male employees, and it was always a different one.

I see people sleeping on the job when they should be working. I've seen on the computer I can see them gambling.

One time I was washing windows, and I saw a man waiting behind the door with a gun to kill someone. I tapped on the window and said what are you doing? He saw me and put up the gun and ran out the room.

One time I was washing windows of a conference room, and it was a man that had two women. Both of the women was all over him, taking off his clothes and their clothes at the same time, really going at it. One of the girls saw me and closed the curtain. Then I move over to the next window. By this time the girls did not have anything on. They never look at me in this window, so I took a break. They went on for hours, but I didn't stay long.

Now this is the best. I was washing windows at a bank. I look in and it was getting robbed so I call the police on my cell phone. I told them I was a window washer, and I was outside and what was going on. Some car was close. I told them if they were quite they could catch the robbers when they came out the door. So they got there, did what I told them to do, and they caught them as soon as they came out of the Bank – problem solved.

I was washing windows. I saw the waitress pretty girl. I looked at her and waved my hands and she waved back. So after I finish I went in and got paid. I asked her name. We talk for a while, I said when do you get off? She said I'm off now. I just work breakfast and sometimes lunch, but if we're busy, I'm in school. Well can I take you out or something? Ok I would like that she said. The next day we had dinner then went to the movies. Five months later we were married. I still do windows. She's in college about to finish. Then we're going to get a window washing business. She's getting a degree in Business Management. We're going to do it together. It all started being a window washer – problem solved.

Now this was a day I will never forget. I was washing windows. I was on top of a twenty store building. It was a man standing on top of the building. I said what are you doing? He said get away and stay away from me. I'm going to jump. Hey can't we talk about this? NO, I have talked enough; my wife is leaving me and taking the children. I have nothing else to live for. I said take a smoke with me. Go away I don't even smoke. Ok I'll smoke one; just tell what you're going through. I sat down right there where he was standing and I listen. First he said she was bipolar; she flies off the handle over anything all the time. I can't take it anymore. I said do she work? He said NO. You make all the money? He said YES. Then where is she going without money? He said well I didn't think about that. I said hey the problem is solved. He went back home and started making sure she takes her pills for her bipolar, and since she drove him crazy, he got a lot of butt calls all the time, and she got pregnant again.

If you need a window washed and I can't do it, then it can't be done.

The Taxi Driver

What is a Taxi driver?

One that drives people everywhere they want to go and you pay them for their services.

What do people do in Taxis in New York if they coming from a party? They do a lot of kissing, hugging, feeling all over each other bodies. When they get to their rooms they pass out.

In New York women going to work put on their make up in the taxi. After that they put on their panty hose. They put on their pony tail then she ready for work – problem solved – pay the TAXI DRIVER.

In Chicago if you want a Taxi you go outside raise your hand. A Taxi will pull up. You tell them where you want to go. Get there, pay the Taxi driver, but make sure it's where you wanted to go before you pay them – problem solved.

This story is in Las Vegas. It was an early night. This man flags me down. How much to get to L. A.? I said that a long way. I'll put you on the meter; you just pay the cost of ending fare. He said sure let's go riding. I said are you in a hurry? I won some money just want to get home. I said Ok we're out of here. One hour meter $110.00 then two hours $220.00. I said where do you live? At 1001 Victory Boulevard in San Bernardino, California. We get there the meter says $330.00. He said here's $400.00 keep the change. I said hey how much did you win? $1,500,000; the rest will go to the bank with an armored truck – problem solved.

This is the day at the airport Nashville. The lady flagged me down at the airport. Take me to Opry Land Hotel. I said is everything Ok? She said everything is great. We are on our way. We get there I looked around. She said wait I'll be right back. She gets out and came right back. Now take me to the Double Tree Hotel downtown Nashville. I said the meter says $34.55. No problem. I said OK downtown Nashville here we come. We hit the interstate no traffic get to the Double Tree downtown. She said be right back. She goes in and comes right back. Take me to the airport. OK, I said, the meter says $72.55 so I hit the interstate, very little traffic. I said are you Ok? Anything wrong? NO everything is perfect. We get to the airport she says let me out the same place you picked me up. The meter said $98.99. I told her what the meter said $98.99. She said Ok and gave me $200.00 and said keep the change. I said what do you do? I deliver diamonds for people when they get expensive ones and they want them handed to them. Most of the time when I deliver, it's for a wedding and they don't trust the mail – problem solved.

If a Taxi takes you to the wrong place do you have to pay them? NO the taxi has to take you to the exact place you want to go in order to be paid. What if they take you back to where they pick you up? You deserve a new Taxi and a different company – problem solved.

The Taxi story in Nashville. I got a call from 2703 Clare Ave. Nashville, Tennessee. Lady comes out with her bag in hand walking like my God you're going to have a baby. I jump out to help her in the car. Take me to Meharry Hospital Emergency. We got on the way; we get to Jefferson Street. She started to scream. She said my water just broke. I said my God it smells like something is happening; we'll be there in two minutes. She was screaming and said I don't have that long. We get to the Hospital. I park at the emergency entrance right next to an ambulance and everything. I run inside, I said she's having a baby outside in my Taxi. It was too late. They start working in my Taxi. Blood was going everywhere; the baby was coming out. Then it start to crying. I said great. Now get ready; there's two babies coming. I almost passed out. Get me a wheel chair. They tried to roll me in the Hospital. I said No I want to stay. Another baby was crying. Now two were born in my Taxi. Two months later I went by to see the family. Her husband was home from the Army. They showed me the babies - two boys. They said we named one of them after you. I said how did you know my name? We got it from the Hospital; they had to help you. You kept passing out, Charles. The first is Charles and the second is Charlie. And you still owe me for the meter fare. No that's OK. I was just joking. You're welcome to see the boys at any time. I held the one named Charles Frost. If you need to go anywhere, I got CHA and it's on me. In Taxis that happened – another problem solved.

The Astronaut

What is an Astronaut?

It is a person that travels in outer space, like the ones on TV in the space movies Scotty beam me up.

If I was an Astronaut I would have to have two girl Astronauts so I would not be alone in outer space – problem solved.

If I was to run into some Aliens we could e=mail each other anytime, as long as I don't have to go through one of those one hour disappearances for hours, and then it looks like two minutes have gone by.

Scotty can you get us out of here? I'm doing the best I can Captain. Well give it all you got; she'll make it. All right Sulu warp seven; let's get the hell out of here before those Klingons show up. You know Captain they stink and they eat weird things. They even like to eat worms.

As you know we travel the Galaxies to discover new things. We put our lives on the line with every ship, every Planet, every Alien forum. We use a computer program for sex protection with Aliens with Butt Calls. The women what they do with Aliens that a different story – problem solved.

As we get farther away from earth, Computer can you get me a wife? Sure Captain. Internet service can you get Mrs. Kurk on line? I can put you on hold; she will be with you after butt call. Captain Kurk she's busy, very busy at the moment. Ya I heard. Sulu turn this ship around. I just been gone five years, she could not wait. Now I got a lot to say about this. Sulu warp ten. YES Sir we'll be back to earth in one hour.

Hey Mother we're going out to play spaceship and Aliens. Lunch will be ready; don't go too far. Hey Ricky were them Aliens? Arrick said they're over there. Hello Mr. and Mrs. Aliens. Beep, beep, beep. What did they say Ricky? I don't know. Eric found them. Where did he go to? He went to get a camera to take their picture. Come on Eric take our picture. OK I have to set the timer so the flash will work right. Ok we got it. Mama got lunch ready and I'm hungry. What y'all got is hot dogs and chips and cold drinks. Alright can the Aliens come? Ask them. Mr. and Mrs. would you want to come to lunch with us? Beep, Beep, Beep. I guess that means YES.

Story

We were heading to a S.O.S. call to a planet they called WHAT'S UP. We heard about it, but never been there. Never seen it at all. We got us a SOS call; the computer checked the location. It was in the Galaxy next to the Milky way, we know that much. I said Victoria how long will it take to get there? She said Captain Eric it will take nine-ten hours. Pilot Eric Jr., put the ship in warp nine. I'm going to check with the Engineers Arrick and Ricky to make sure the ship in good shape for this trip. Arrick and Ricky what the problem is?

We just rocking and rolling down here. Ya that's what y'all always doing since you got those two lady engineers down there with you to help on repairs. Now I see why you keep bugging me to get y'all some help. We got a SOS call from a planet What's Up. Captain we're going to put in some engine cleaner. It will only take ten seconds and we can hit warp 1000 if you want to. I'm cool with that. Victoria what did the computer say about that planet? As much as for now, Captain Eric, all I got is it is inhabited and does have life form. That's all I got for now.

Well I think we need to talk to Home Base. Get General Dennise Cunningham on the line. Will do Captain Eric Cunningham. Thank you, Victoria Cunningham. Computer get me Home Base on earth. Hello you have Home Base. This is Phyllis, system control specialist, how can I help you? This is ship Galaxy Star. We are in route to a SOS call to a Planet What's Up. Captain Eric wants to confirm with General Dennise Cunningham how everything is at Home Base.

Phyllis said everything here same as always till we got your call, Victoria. Here comes the General. This is the General. What's going on out there, Captain Eric and crew? We got a SOS call from a planet What's Up. A what call, Captain Eric? What is tomorrow? Friday. OK tomorrow is Friday and what else is tomorrow? Think hard, Captain Eric. Well just my birthday.

Gotcha, Gotcha, Gotcha. We all Gotcha. There's no SOS call and who would name a planet What's Up? That's something you always say, What's up. Happy birthday in advance. Me, Phyllis and Phinne we are putting together something for you. Just make it to Home Base tomorrow. By our time a big party will be set for you. Just act surprised. We got you good this time, Little Brother. I'm going to get you back, Big Sister. I'm the General you can't get me back. SOS we got the Captain Little Brother out in space, anything can happen. So if you get a SOS call, make sure it's a real SOS call.

Well, we got a party to go to. Little Eric turn this ship around and head to Home Base. Take it slow; we are in no hurry. Out in space anything can happen. Eric Jr. warp two. Just take us home; we have a party to go to.

The Forest Ranger

What is a Forest Ranger?

A person that patrols the forest for fires, illegal hunting, to help people in danger. Smokey the Bear is one of the best.

Thank you for watching *We Got a Question*. Mr. Eric Cunningham are you ready? What would you do if a big Grizzly Bear jumped on your car? If I was not in it, I would walk away as fast as I could, then run like hell for dear life. That was a good answer you win a thousand dollars.

If you were out camping and a pack of wolves ran up on you, what would you do? First I would say God have I been a good man to make it to heaven, because I think I am on the way if these wolves are hungry. That was a good answer you win a thousand dollars.

Next Question – you are asleep. A load noise wakes you up. You see a blazing fire outside your tent. What would you do? First I would look to see if I'm surrounded, if not I would grab things I need to survive with. I would get as much as I could in the time that I have. I would surely have camped by water and would get there as quickly as possible. If the fire was not on the other side of the water I would work to get to the other side of the water and call the Forest ranger for help and give my location. That is another great answer you win another thousand dollars.

One more question. If you answer one more question you win ten thousand dollars. Here is the question.

You and your friends are going to a resort to ski and going up a very high mountain road with thousands of feet drop off on your passenger side, and your car cut off. You can't get it started. It's getting dark and it's two degrees below freezing. What would you do? First I would try to get it started, ask my friends if they have any mechanical experience, make sure the car was secured, turn on my emergency lights so people could see the car and we needed help. Get on my phone to see if we could get some on the road help from AAA. I have that insurance. Let's check with the judges and see. Mr. Cunningham they give you the winnings. Here is your check for ten thousand. Altogether Mr. Cunningham you have won thirteen thousand dollars.

Hey we've got a question and thank you ladies and gentleman for watching *We Got A Question.*

This is the story of a Forest Ranger, Mr. Leroy Cuningham, this was a call from a women that lives right at the boarder of the forest. She and her family have five acres of land. Residential area fenced in to keep control of the wild animals and big bears from getting out of the forest into peoples land. Everyone new about that big Grizzly Big Joe. He was the oldest Grizzly around. People knew about him. He was way out of his feeding zone. He roamed mostly down by the river that was about twenty miles from the area around where the border fence-line was. We got to the lady's house. She had two kids. They meet us at the gate. They saw Big Joe walking around way out in the field. They called us and got into their SUV to stay safe and get far away, but they could still see Big Joe. Our team got together; it was nine of us. There were four rangers and three policemen and two firemen. Big Joe was walking toward the house. We stayed by the house out of sight so we could tranquilize that Big Joe and take him back home. We stayed very low so Big Joe would not see us because it would scare him off and it would be harder to catch him. He never saw us so he kept on coming toward the house. He got close enough to the house that we got a shot off. It hit him but he turned and ran. We got another shot in Big Joe, as he was trying to get away.

He slowed down and then he stopped and sat down. That meant the medicine was taking effect. In five minutes Big Joe was taking a nap. We pumped him with enough shots to keep him asleep for at least five-six hours and that would be enough time to get him loaded in the truck and get him back home.

After we got him back to his home by the river, we left him twenty pounds of meat so he would have something to eat after he woke up. This was not the first time we had to give Big Joe a little ride. We watched him with our binoculars where he could not see us. He woke up and looked around for about an hour then he ate what we left and then problem solved.

Another story was a Lumber Jack was taking his wife to the hospital to have a baby. The car broke down. We had just left the hospital. Over the radio we was on the same channel. We were even on the same road. As we headed to the call, we looked at the problem. We stopped and helped the lady and she was fine. We put her and her friend in our SUV. Her husband followed in his truck. We headed to the hospital and were lucky that the lady wasn't in labor. We called back two days later to check on her. She had a little girl and everything was fine. OK problem solved by the FOREST RANGERS.

The Singers

What are singers?

They make music with their voices, perform by singing. It costs an arm and a leg to see them but it is always worth it.

We have some stars here and we're going to ask them all one question to see what each of them would say.

The question is. If you could change the world what would you do?

Mr. James Brown the God-Father of Soul. Well I feel good. The first thing is no more wars, no more killing in the streets. People would help and love each other. No more drugs in the street; it got to go. Love God and everyone live in peace. We going to have a big Bar-B-Q tomorrow. Everyone is invited till all the food is gone. If we need some more, I will buy some more.

Ms. Whitney Houston. Everyone to praise God, Jesus and the Holy Spirit. First I love you all. No more homeless people, no more hungry people in the world, everyone in the world will have a good education. Everyone will have love and peace for each other. I am helping on the Bar-B-Q so scurry down to the stone Soul picnic.

Michael Jackson, What up? We got the King of Rock. What's your word, Michael Jackson? I want the world to be free of people being locked up, with love and peace and happiness. All the animals to be able to run free and go anywhere. The people holding hands singing songs. We are God's children of the world. Make this safe for everyone and everyone give God praises. The Bar-B-Q I'm in on that. I'll bring some veg. Burgers for the people that don't eat meat.

Mahalia Jackson, what's on your mind, Mrs. Jackson? I want to help the children to see peace in the world. It is the power of God. Everyone to open their hands and help each other all the time. No more crime in the world, no more poverty. Let communication be with love and understanding. If someone says help give them a hand. Let God show you the way for peace, love and souls in the world. I'm going to make some fried chicken and corn bread for the Bar-B-Q tomorrow.

The Question is, If you could change the world what would you do?

Mr. Prince, love in the whole world with peace, love and no more war; no guns no more killing. The world to love and live in peace to make it safe for everyone. All the children to be safe and have a good education. God is on our side; the world will be on Gods side, with love for everyone with peace in their heart. At the Bar-B-Q I'll be performing there. Just tell what you want us to bring.

Are you ready for Mimi Ripperton? Mrs. Ripperton, you look beautiful. What do you have for the world? From my heart love, love and more love, peace. No more hungry people in the world. No more pollution, no more sickness, no more cancer, no more HIV. Just a great clean world. No more guns, no more drugs, just a happy peaceful, loving world. Is the Bar-B-Q today or tomorrow? What do I need to do? I love to cook. I have children.

Are you ready for Berry White the Maestro of Music? In your words, Mr. White, tell us about your world. Thank you for having me here. The first thing I would do is make the people have love for each other all over the world. No more guns, no wars, then you have peace, love and soul for all the people. Show the children love, love and more love. No more people locked up in jail or prison. The whole world communicating with love with God, Jesus and the Holy Spirit leading the way. God can make our future great with peace, love and the Soul. That Bar-B-Q tomorrow, just e-mail on what you want me to bring.

And last but not least, Donna Summers, the Queen of Disco. You ready, Ms. Summers. I am. Tell us about your world. First of all, thank you for having me here, and first of all, it's God world. I would love for everyone to help keep it clean, be happy and take care of each other with love, hope and carrying. No drugs, no sickness with beautiful smiling faces with love, love, and more love. No hunger with extra love all over the world. Did I say that already? No bombs and people helping each other. Oh yeah, what's up with that Bar-B-Q. I want to help. Just text me to tell what you want me to bring.

The Actor

What is an Actor?

People and animals, some time you have cartoons that act. They do plays, movies and films and some get famous.

If I could have been an actor, I would love to have been on that western Bonanza working with the Cartwright family on the Ponderosa and been a cowboy. Yee haa!

The *High Chaparral* is one of my favorite westerns. I would have loved to be an actor on that show as a cowboy working with Monlito and Buck, Blue boy solving the problems of that wild west desert, with Apache Indians. Some time they were trouble, sometimes they work together to solve some of the problems.

I have always liked magic and to be an actor on the show *Bewitched*. I would love to one of the Magic people on that show to do anything magical. That was good like a Warlock friend of the family or an assistant to that witch Doctor that always came to the rescue of Samantha Stevens. What really trips me out was that lady across the street that always saw them do things with magic but she never could prove it.

There is another show that was very funny and it was *Mork and Mindy*. It is so funny with an Alien from outer space. It was so funny word for word everything. He would say Arc this and Arc that and how he reported back to his home planet. It was so funny, how he would explain the things that was going on on earth.

I wonder whose the voice was of the Alien that was a leader. He had to talk to from his home planet. I'd like to say God bless Robin Williams. I would have loved to meet him face to face because he was a great man.

As we take off in *Star Trek* that Ship the Enterprise, I would love to live on something like that in real life. That was a real job, and how to deal with the Aliens that is a big question, because if you can't communicate with them or the right words when you meet them, how could you keep from getting killed or kill them? Let's say you say hello and in that language that may mean lets have sex to the other Aliens. So I say, whenever we get to the point that we are in outer space, that there be a good thing and we get along with them and we start out in peace to solve our problems. So let's explore the Galaxy and live in peace.

This would be a dream come true and we would live happily ever after. I would do anything to make a movie with Pam Grier. I loved her dearly. If I could have done a movie with her, I would take any part just to see her face to face and be her friend, husband, son, cousin. Anything to be with her. My name is Eric Marton Cunningham. I love you and always will, Pam Grier, my movie star – problem solved.

Now 007 is an actor. I would love to be a 007 before I leave this earth if God is willing. I would like to play a part in one of those movies especially the fast action parts. They always have a lot of live action in all of the 007 James Bond movies, and don't forget the beautiful ladies. Either they were going to kill him or help him or make love to him always in his movies. It's like this.

You sitting on the edge of your seat. Your eyes never blink because you might miss something. All the actors that have played 007 I SALUTE YOU. A JOB WELL DONE – ANOTHER PROBLEM SOLVED.

One of my most favorite movies with black actors was *Buck and the Preacher*. I loved westerns. *Posey* was a good movie. It too was one with a lot of black actors. One day I would like to be in one of those wild westerns with some of those foxy ladies. Well, pulling guns, bang, bang, that was real acting.

The *Andy Griffith Show* I would love to have been in some of his shows like working with Goober the mechanic at the gas station. Being one of the Highway Patrolmen that shows up with a prisoner to stay overnight. Come to Mayberry to find a prisoner that has got away from prison, or have to look after Otis who had a bad night and have to sleep it off. I always wondered if there really was a Mayberry, North Carolina.

This is a salute to Richard Pryor. I would have loved to have worked with this great man, to me the King of Comedy. Any movie he made I would love to have been in. It has been great to just watch his work as an actor. I salute you, Sir. You were a great man; you left the world a lot to look at.

To all the Actors in the world, My name is Eric Marton Cunningham. May God bless you in your work. I Salute all. Good luck in your acting life. Amen.

The Movie Star

What is a Movie Star?

The actors that play in movies, plays or films and they are the main attraction can be a person, animal or a cartoon, that everyone wants to see.

Opra Winfrey is a very great movie star that I see in movies. She has played parts in movies, she has a great career in the entertainment world. The Opra Winfrey show is always a great show to watch. It is educational, was on for many decades and the people that went to the show always received a very good gift for attending. As a guest on her show it would be very rewarding in many ways. She is one of Nashville, Tennessee's greatest people, and we are proud of Opra. She also graduated from Tennessee State University in Nashville, Tennessee. We love you and we salute you for a Job well done. May you HAVE A BLESSED DAY EVERY DAY. You are truly a woman of God's Gold.

Another movie star I am very impressed with is Billy DEE Williams, a smooth talking black man that hit the movie screen and became the lady's man who is down with the brothers. He has been in so many movies it's hard to remember them all. *Lady Sings the Blues* with Dina Ross. I salute her too. She is a great singer and actor. In *Star Wars* Billy had a great part and was very impressive, he was in the *Under Cover Brother* he had a great roll in that movie with that funny man Eddie Griffin. He has a great future in Comedy and movies. I salute him too. To all the actors out there, I salute you.

Your day will come. Just keep working and be in the right place at the right time – problem solved.

Ms. Pam Grier, I loved every movie you made. If it's coming I'm watching. For Pam Grier, put her on cable and I would watch her till my screen burned out. To me you are the most beautiful woman in my world. All the movies you made I have watched them because you were in them, and they were great, and you just look too good to pass up. It seems that you don't get older you get younger, Pam Grier. I, Eric Marton Cunningham, salute you. May God bless you today and every day you filming. I'm watching you.

Eddie Griffin is a great movie star, comedian, actor, great on stage with comedy. The movie *Undercover Brother* was magnificent. Mr. 007 has nothing on you. I look forward to the next movie. Just make it better. That one was great. Your comedy on stage act was too good to talk about. You got the super skills to bring out laughter. You are a young black man; you have a great future. In the entertainment business, your future has no limit. You can go far. Stay focused. You can go higher and higher. Just keep working – problem solved.

Zsa Zsa Gabor a very beautiful lady, a marvelous actress in *Green Acres*, that most beautiful lady out in the country, very funny with coffee thick as ice cream, with pan cakes that bobbled. With a closet that was never closed, with a telephone that you had to climb a pole to talk on. Even with all these problems Zsa Zsa made it all worth watching *Green Acres*. All the people on that show did great work on the people they played, even Arnold the pig. Zsa Zsa may God bless you always for the great work you did as a movie star.

Michael Landon was a major movie star better known as Little Joe on *Bonanza*. That is a great show that comes on as a western family on the Ponderosa with the big ranch and all the money. Michael is a super actor had some great shows, *The Little House on the Prairie*, and many more. Never got married on the Bonanza show; was always the person on the rescue for the people in need. That was a good thing to see to give yourself the feeling that you can also be a good person to help someone in need. You're a great man, Michael Landon. God bless you as a movie star.

Charley Sheen *Two and a Half Men*. That is a super funny show. It's always a good show to watch even if you watch the same shows over and over again. Charley Sheen is a big movie star. He has class even if he looks like he drinks a lot, make love to a lot of women. His style is so cool that he gets away with doing wrong but make it OK, in his way of living. They have a great performance on every show, even his mother. She has a great part in the family; they have a strange kind of family. Although they are always there when they need each other, almost like the *Adams Family*, you never know what to expect. Charley, a great show. Keep up the great work. You are the funny man; great show – another problem solved.

The Stunt Man

What is a Stunt Man?

A person that does the dangerous things in the entertainment business making movies, plays and films. He or she takes the place of the movie star in the dangerous scenes.

The movie star is in a car and right at the end of the races he's about to win, he loses control of the car and it crashes into a wall and blows up. They change the star to a stunt man – problem solved.

This is a bar room. The movie star's talking to a beautiful lady; they're long lost friends. He does not know she is married now they run into each other. They hug each other. She did not say she was married now. Her jealous husband sees them hugging. The movie star change to the stunt man The husband beats him up all over the bar. Then she tells her husband that they're old friends from college. They just ran into each other. Be careful who you hug; it could cost you.

Two girls meet. They work at the same place. They get to talking about their boyfriends. Little do they know they're dating the same man. He is supposed to meet one of the ladies there not knowing that both of the ladies are there. The man is the star of the movie playing a big shoot. One of the ladies goes to the ladies' room. The lady he is to meet is still there. He meets her and they greet each other. He kisses her. At the same time the other lady comes out of the ladies room and see them KISSING. After coming out of the ladies' room, she says You're kissing my man. And the other lady says now he's my man. Then the star changes to a stunt man, and the two ladies beat the crap out of the man for two timing those two ladies.

This lady is a U.S. Spy. She is under cover in the drug deal to catch the big boss. Little does she know they have done a background check and they know who she is. She comes in with the money to make the buy and get them on tape making the drug deal. The boss does not play the game. She expects them to play the game; she comes in and everything falls apart. Then they change the Star to a stunt lady for her. The boss, the Mr. Big, tells his boys to take her out to the sea and put here in a boat and blow her up. They do what the Big Boss says with her. They get her out there, leave her in a little boat and blow it up. As they are leaving her, she jumps out before it blows up. She gets another shot at them.

Wild West, the big showdown. The Cunningham Brothers. It's four of them coming back home from prison. They served two years for a crime they did not comet. They get back home. The ranch has been taken by the Jones family, the one that framed them. They get to the ranch with guns in their faces. The Jones say get off this land; it belong to Jones now. The Cunninghams say this is not the last of this. We will be back, and they ride out. They get to town, go to see the Sheriff. He says boys I can't help you. The Jones are running the Town. The Sheriff says, just leave town. It will be safe for you, and go to another town and start over. The Cunninghams said our family has been working that land for four generations. That almost two hundred years. We made that land what it is. We're not going to give it up just because we were gone for two years for a crime we did not even commit. We even made this town. The people if they needed anything, we helped them and did not ask for anything in return. For those five hundred head of cows, we paid for them. They framed us with the killing of those men that brought those cows here, and they stole the bill of sale. We had it. So they sent the Jones a note. You have two days to clear out. You know you framed us, and we will not give up that easy. Two days the stunt men took the stars', the Cunningham's, places. They came with their guns blazing. The town people heard that the Cunninghams needed help to get their land back. So a hundred men came with them to get their land back because while the Cunningham's where gone some of the Jones had told what really went down. They were drunk and was laughing at the Cunninghams. They got to the Cunningham's house and the Jones saw what they were up against and dropped their guns, and gave the Cunningham's their land back. They always said when you do things to help people they will be there to help you – another problem solved.

It was a beautiful day. Everyone was at the big boat race in downtown Nashville, Tennessee, on the Cumberland River down by the riverfront. It will start at the Opryland Mall; it will be televised on Channel 5. Twenty of the best boaters in the world. The finish line will be at the RIVERFRONT downtown Nashville. Everything is set. The race with some star boat divers. The race started.

They were flying loud boats, water with waves almost five feet high when they made turns going super-fast. They got to the finish line 1, 2, 3, 4, 5. The sixth boat hit a wave. The star was replaced with a stunt-man. The boat rolled over four times and landed upside down and was floating. They got the driver out; he recovered. A OK.

The Comedian

What is a Comedian?

They are people that make you laugh. They are funny; some are hilarious. Some put on faces like clowns; some use tools like a doll and use voice control. There are so many ways, and it's all about just being funny.

My Name is Eric Marton Cunningham. My stage name is Sir Eric The Cunningham. I've been on *Soul Train*, I have been in movies *The Big Man On Campus*. I have done T.V. Commercials for a Nissan Dealership, Colletto Nissan in California. Now I want to be a Comedian.

So what the problem is, can I make people laugh? Well I have been doing it all my life.

What the problem with men and women? With women its men. Men, if you want to get out of being a yes man, then be an OK man. If your wife ask for some money then you say OK. That gives you time to think if she don't hit you up side your head and throw her hand out again. But if she don't, just say, Baby I'm thinking, and she will say thinking about what? And you say if you going to take all my money. Then she going to say don't I always give you something for it? And then you say OK I want a lot of Butt calls tonight, Ok? That's how an Ok man gets problem solved.

Ladies would you like to be an alright woman instead of a yes women? So when he asks for some SEX say alright. Then he is going to say come on I'm ready. Then you say I'm thinking. He is going to say thinking about what? How we going to do it. I want to do it different than the way we did it different. So by now, saying that, he should have a smile on his face. He's thinking of something new. So now ladies you're not a yes women. You are a alright women and you get to have sex – different problem solved.

If you could have sex with a pretty women or an ugly women who would you choose? An ugly woman. They are more active and pleasing than a pretty woman. The ugly women will keep you around longer too.

If you could have sex with a tall lady or a short lady, who would you pick? Tall ladies are demanding, short ladies, they do everything, and they like a lot of attention too.

If you could have sex with all the women in the world, how many would it be? All of them.

Women, if you could have sex with all the men in the world how many would it be? All the ones that have a Job because it would not be FREE.

If you could have sex with a rich ugly women or a poor beautiful woman, I would take the rich one. Then I could buy the sex from the beautiful one.

How do you know a girl like you? When you look at her and she look back when you smile and she smile. When you walk over and say hello, and she says hello back with a man voice, that's not a girl.

If you were in a Club how would you know what girl would like to go home with you? First you have to see the girl you like. When you find her you go over and talk to her. Be real cool and nice to the other girls as well the ones she sitting with. You talk to the girl you like and then get her away to talk in private if possible. If she comes away with you, you're half way there.

How long do you know a girl before you have sex? After you have spent some money on her she owes you something. Time to pay up.

When is the best time to get real with a girl after you have had sex with her? If it's good, she good – problem solved.

Is sex the only things girls are good for? They just think that all men want it from them. That's when you run to a girl that can cook.

If two girl want to have sex with you what do you do? Be very careful. Don't let them pick the location because if you go in, you may not come out – problem solved.

8.

Sports

Football	184
Fishing	186
Basketball	189
Track & Field	192
Soccer	195
Tennis	198
Hockey	201
Horse Racing	204

Football

What is Football?

It is a sport that you have to get a touch down or a field goal to score a point to win. How do you win? Don't lose.

Who are the ones that are playing? Everyone on the field. There are two teams and only one can win and one can lose. The best team wins. Which one do you want?

What do they do to knock each other out? Block and tackle all the game. The ones that does it best win. You still have to pick one.

Can any one play football? YES and NO, Yes if you can stand getting beat up and blocked and getting knocked out, and NO if you can't stand the pain.

Football, football, football. Everyone like football. Is there anything better? Let me see. NO.

Can children play football? YES, any time their mother is not around.

Is football a good game? It is the best game in the world. You go to it to have fun, eat hot dogs, drink a lot of beer, and pass out.

Can women play football? YES in the bedroom. Get the football, get naked, and it turns into a butt call.

Can you watch it on TV? YES with a room full of people screaming so loud that they almost tear your wall down, full of beer and waking up the neighborhood.

Football is a game of power, speed and skills at all times – even in your back yard for kids only.

Is football like a job? YES, you can get paid if you go PRO. What is that? It's when people buy tickets to a game that will cost you a whole pay check for a ticket.

What is a game? When the men are playing football and the ladies cheer leading in skirts and all the men wishing they could get one of the cheerleaders for a butt call.

The Super Bowl what is that? It's the game with the two best football teams. How do you get a Ticket? Win the Powerball.

How do you become a good football player? If you start now you can be one in twenty years.

Is football everywhere? YES, you can play it in your back yard; you can play it in the park; they play it in school; they play it so much they go PRO.

Is it OK for girls to play football? YES and NO. Yes if they play with shorts pants on and they have big hooters. If not, NO.

What is a touch down? It's when you cross the goal line and get six points. The teams try to do it every time. If they don't they lose – big problem.

Football is the way to go. It's a lot of fun everybody knows. To win the game is part of the fun and getting mixed up is part of the fun, and don't forget the winning team gets a Butt Call.

Fishing

What is fishing?

A sport that people buy boats, fishing supplies to catch the biggest fish or the most in weight. Some catch them to eat them.

Fishing is fun. If you go and don't catch anything you can always go to the store and buy some and say you caught them, but don't forget to thaw them out.

Fishing is great, especially the story about the one that got away. It was a giant and every time you tell the story the fish gets bigger.

Everyone has a giant fish story. What if I almost caught JAWS but he ate someone else? So we throw him back – problem solved.

I almost caught MOBY DICK but I woke up.

I was fishing on the bank of the river. I could not get a bite for hours. I saw a man out in a little boat just catching one every time he cast out his line. I asked him how he was catching so many fish. He said I will have to show you. So he came to the bank and said you have to buy a boat, then tell them to put glass at the bottom of your boat. That why I catch so many. I can look down at the water and see the fish and tell where the fish are – PROBLEM SOLVED.

A story has a good ending especially when you are the only one there.

The one that got away is the Americas favorite, except now when you go, and the people have cell phones, and the phone never lies.

I think it's a shame when you throw out a little fish to catch a big fish, except your little fish catch you a big fish and now you see the mouth of JAWS trying to get the big fish the little fish got you. What a story that would be.

I like to fish. You're out in the wild with nature, the water and the fresh air. All of a sudden a big bear runs you away from your spot. Then you see a sign that says for BEARS ONLY.

It's a great day to fish. Everyone is catching fish but me. I'm using the best bait, and it is very quiet, so I asked them how are you catching so many fish. They said this is a stocked lake. You fish with hook only.

As the world of sports covers a great fish meet, today we have the winner. How many fish did you catch? He said two. How did you win? I was the only one here. Everyone thought the meet was for tomorrow.

The seafood world is served by the fishing world. Sometime the food is old seafood in the stores, so check the expiration date. It may be old – another problem solved.

Some people love to fish. They catch fish to give it away sometimes. Now that's good; you will not have to go to the store and buy any. If it's on Friday, it right on time.

In some places they have fish that will jump into your boat, but some fish will make you jump out of your boat.

Fishing has been around for years. People catch fish with poles, nets, fishing rods, and some people catch fish with their hands. They are still looking for some of those people.

I would like to catch a really big fish like my Uncle. We got a picture of the fish; still looking for my Uncle.

The world is full of great fishermen. The only thing they never show you is where they caught those big giant fish.

Basketball

What is Basketball?

It is a great sport people play, where they try to get the ball in a basket any way possible. Most of the time its tall people.

Basketball is the name of the game that people try to get the ball in the hoop as fast as you can; they check all the people man to man. They try to get the highest points as fast as you can. If you don't, you lose. What is losing? You don't WIN.

Basketball everyone loves it. All you're doing is shooting the ball through that round HOOP. Is it fun? YES if they ever give you the ball.

What do you shoot the ball with? Anything but a gun.

Are all the people shooting in the same hoop? NO, sometime they have two hoop whole court, at separate ends of the court so you run a lot. You win or you pass out.

Can any one play? YES, children, teenagers, grown people. But where? The park, school, college anywhere you see a hoop. What if you don't have a ball? You're out of luck.

I heard that people even JAM the ball. What is that? You make ball go in hoop without shooting the ball.

How do you do that? JAM, first grow tall a lot. Then you take the ball up to the hoop and slam it in with all your might. I did it good once, but I had a ladder.

Shoot, Shoot, Shoot the hoop. That was a great game you won. YES, it would have been a great game if the other team had showed up.

Have the basketball been around long? YES, we had a lot of tall people, so we had to find something for them to do.

Everyone comes in. The game is on. That's the life you live at the sports bar. Lots of people, men & women, beer, hot wings, for all this - a game. What if your team loses? Then you wish you had not came.

All teams lose sometimes, but for a team that always wins, although there are teams that always lose. When they win they get upset.

Basketball is a sport for the fast, the tall, the skilled, the fast of foot. What if you fast play football – problem solved.

Is basketball for year round? YES, except the PROs. They only play when they are getting paid.

If I was a basketball player, I would retire and be a player and get a lot of Butt Calls.

To be a baller that is the question. A person that play basketball, do they work? YES, day in day out. The baller, do they eat? Maybe. Do they sleep? Maybe. Are they on drugs? Maybe. Then what do they do? THEY GET A LOT OF Butt CALLS.

Basketball players, you play with your ball, you sleep with your ball, you run around with your ball, you hoop with your ball. Just marry your ball.

The day I found that basketball, it was just sitting there. I pick it up they said shoot it. I said where is the hoop? I shot it and it went in. I been hooping every since. That was twenty years ago.

As time goes on the game getting better. The people are getting taller. The places they play are getting better. I think I'm going to stop because that is getting too good. I think it is a set up for something. Nothing should be that good.

Basketball it's one thing. That Championship game, the best team wins and then you have the world Champion basketball team. But the next day you have to wait till next year to see another basketball game.

Track and Field

What is Track and Field?

It is competition people go through to show if they faster then everyone and stronger than everyone, and it's all done by hand and feet.

The fast will be the fastest; the slow will be the slowest; the strong will be the strongest; the weak will be the weakest. The ones in the middle will not get noticed.

The big race the one hundred yard dash. Who will win? We don't know; they have not started yet.

There's always a winner and always loser. What about the second and third place and so on? They still lose; they did not win.

There are a lot of races in track. What is the hardest all of them? After they finish running, they're all burn out and very, very tired.

What about the races with teams and they pass the baton? Now that's when they all walk around burned out and out of breath.

Now let's go to the stuff where they don't run. That's even harder. Lets say weight lifters. The thing they have to pick up is twice their weight. It don't matter who ever pick up the heaviest weight wins. If he picks up a thousand pounds, you have to pick up a thousand and one to win, even if your weight is a hundred and fifty pounds.

The big round ball is the shot put. You get in a circle and spin around and then throw it as far as you can while you are dizzy as hell without stepping out of the circle. Now that is crazy, I mean if you did it.

Now this is out of this world, the pole vault. There is a very thin aluminum line you have to go over without knocking it down, and it is held up by two 16-foot poles. You have to go over that thin aluminum line without knocking it down, by running with a aluminum pole in your hand. It will be and thrown up in the air you have to get over that aluminum line. Good luck.

This is the long, long race distance two miler. That's around the track eight times I would be through after the first time. Second time, are you crazy?

Now this is always the last race of the track meet, the mile relay. Everyone in the race has to go around the track one time and pass the baton to a team mate. Here's how it goes: start fast, go around the first turn you're ok, you're on the back straight away still Ok. You get to the next turn your legs start to get heavy. It feels like you just gained fifty pounds. You push on, you make the turn. Now the monkey is on your back. It's like you have fifty more pound on your back. All you can do is think about the finish line or pass that baton. After that, all that is on your mind is 911 help.

There are a lot of things that go on in a track meet. One is the long jump. This is a seventy foot sprint and then you step on a line. Then you jump, as far as you can in the air, and land in the sand. You move forward out of the sand. They measure your mark. Then you see how far you were flying. This is your best because the running in the races will kill you, and you can win in the long jump. You can win or lose in every competition, so win every time.

Run, Run this is a good track. The only thing about the track after you run on it, you hate it if you lose, but you love the track if you win.

The start of the season, the first meet. That's what they call the event, a training meet. If you win you are doing great in training. You just have to keep that passion for the season. If you lose you have to build your strength in your body to be better. You can do anything to be better except steroids.

The new race – you always want to know is any one faster than you? If they are, the best thing for you to do is to think about win, win, win, win enough. Though you always come in last, you could feel winning for a little while.

Losers can always become winners. They just have press on or find a better coach.

Soccer

What is Soccer?

It is a sport played men and women where they have to kick a ball in a goal that's set on the ground about eight feet high and fifteen feet wide. You have to kick the ball in the goal to get points to win. The field is as big as Yellow Stone National Park.

The field is so big, if you go to one side and back that's almost a half mile. For this sport you have to train cross country.

There's not much scoring in this sport. You could win with one point, if the other team don't get two.

You kick the ball with any part of your body except your hands. The goaly is the only one that can use his hands to catch the ball to stop points for the other team.

There are so many words to put in this game. I know one – win the game.

You can kick the ball anyway you can to make it go in the goal, and it has to get past that man in front of the goal, while he is looking right at you.

This sport is played all over the world. The United States sometimes they like football.

Soccer Mexican, Latinos, Italians; the Chinese are too short. They would have to rent a goaly.

Do kids play Soccer? If the parents can buy the supplies, health insurance, transport to the game and not kill the referee if someone bumps into their child.

Soccer is a very safe game. Everyone is kicking the ball. If you want the ball you have to kick it. If someone is in the way they get kicked too.

Women play Soccer too. Men like to watch them kick the ball. Their legs go up, so you know what they're looking at.

Fast, quick, fast on your feet. Don't forget you have to run miles to play this game.

Kick the ball in the goal in the air, on the ground. Kick with your feet. If your head is in the way you have a problem. They are kicking at that ball.

This sport has no body protection except on your legs. It guards below your knee, and the ball is there most of the time, so you have a kick fight.

Win, win and win that's the name of this game. They play a long time up and down the field, miles after miles. A whole season they have kicked that ball around the world.

Do children play this game a lot? Sometimes kids in the hood. They're into football, basketball whatever the girls like to look at.

Around the world the Championship comes from everywhere. The best team goes home with a trophy.

Don't forget a lot of running. I think the team that is not tired by now will win.

Do you know any soccer players? This is how they look: slim, tall and small feet. If you find a fat one he is the Coach.

Has soccer been around long? If you're from Europe you would know.

Has the United States ever did well? YES, the ladies WON a Championship; I don't know how it was on the news.

Do they have soccer teams in school? Mostly in college in Europe, Mexico, Italy, The United States maybe.

Tennis

What is Tennis?

It is a sport of hitting a ball over a net. You have to keep the ball inside the squares. A lot of people and children play this game. To watch this game you have a lot of neck work, left to right or right to left.

My salute to Serena and Venus Williams. They have made history for the black women in the world of tennis and these two ladies look beautiful when they play.

Can't keep my eyes on the game you two ladies just look too good, especially when the wind shows your beautiful figure when you're serving or running after the ball.

For Serena and Venus, I think that if you're late, your opponent is happy for a little while. They think you may not show up, but when you walk in, it's over.

Tennis is a lot of running serving the ball and back and forth. You have to be in shape just to watch.

Those William ladies I wish they could play longer. They serve so many Aces you only see them but five minutes of a set, and they don't even sweat.

Tennis is a sport for all ages, young, middle age, old as long as you can run, run with more running and a lot of left and rights you're good to go.

The best players go to Wimbledon and when you get over there, they have people to massage your necks so you can watch the games a lot easier.

These games so fast 15, 30, 40, love, game over, that's one part. That's why the game goes so fast.

Tennis it keeps you in great shape because you run after you serve the ball; you run when they hit it back; you run to hit it back to them. On and on it goes. Don't forget your neck to be in shape to watch.

Fast, fast, fast game run, run, run. That just what you have to do to get to your seat before the game is over.

Oh ya, the only time you don't have to use a lot of neck muscles is when you're watching Tennis on TV. You just need some good EYE muscles.

Ace, the super serve easy point and quick game. When you do that a lot, you don't play many people. They say you're too good to play against.

Win, win, win that what people think about. For people that lose, that is as close as they can get for them to win.

What can a loser do? 1. Say I was there 2. I was part of the game 3. I hope that person that beat me is not here next year.

All games have winners and losers. What about the ones in the middle? This sport don't have a middle. Its one wins or one loses, then game over.

I like the ladies in short skirts, see their beautiful figure. It's even better than a butt call.

All sports have their up and down. Well the Williams, they're more in the upbeat – problem solved.

Serena you win; you are the sexiest sports woman in the world to me. You Ace's so much we can't watch you play. We would like to see you longer, longer and longer. That would be a great game to watch.

The world has Tennis as the greatest sport for the WILLIAMS SISTERS. If you have children, show them the videos of the WILLIAMS SISTERS playing tennis so there will be WILLIAMS FAMILY CHAPTER TWO. Serena and Venus, I Salute you and wish you Blessing Always from Eric Marton Cunningham.

Hockey

What is Hockey?

It is a game people play on ice, where a lot of men fight a lot trying to get a round puck in a goal past the goaly.

They fight all the time. A man gets slammed into the wall and he had a shot at the goal. Then they stop till they put the man that slammed him into the penalty box. Then the game start again; they're back to fighting.

They look great on the ice till they smile; then you see a lot of teeth missing.

Some places they throw things on the ice for certain reasons. In Nashville they throw catfish most of the time. It's about fifteen or twenty pounds. Later you can smell it cooking; it's called a fish fry.

Fight, fight, fight. They fight so much sometimes they win if someone get knocked out. No I'm sorry, that boxing.

They go at it for three periods. Whoever is leading at the end of three periods wins and then they fight over that – problem solved.

One time both teams got to fighting. Both teams was put in the penalty box for two minutes. After they got out, they beat up the referees.

The ice is very slick, impossible to stand on, so they have ice skates, and they are ready. So it's play or fight. That is the Question.

It's a very rough sport. You have to have great balance skills to be on your feet and fast and ready to win, win, win. But if you lose you have to fight, fight and fight because the coach is going to kill you.

Kids play it to although they can't fight because if they do their mothers will get to fighting in the stands because your boy hit her boy. They would fight worse than the PRO'S.

The Nashville Predators went all the way to the STANLEY CUP. We salute you for that.

They got there because they did not lose many fights and won a lot of games.

They outscored a lot of teams to win, but they had a lot of fight to get that far.

The Predators said half way in the season if their fighting skills was down, they was going to recruit Bruce Leroy to give them some ACT RIGHT.

The people in the stands love their team. If other people come in from out of town with the other team it's like war. They try to out drink each other. Most beer wins – problem solved.

Everyone want to have the best team. What if your team always looses? They would have the worst team, then they don't have to fight for that.

The winning team finally brought the winning team to the South. THE NASHVILLE PREDATORS will be ready next year. When they heal up from all those aches and pains from all those fights and the people in the stands come off those hangovers.

Nashville has a great trophy now for TENNESSEE, a big pretty one this trophy. They can keep forever. The STANLY CUP you only get to keep for one year.

Hockey is a man game. The women go to the game so they can find a man that will marry them and so they can get what they want. Then men call their wives from the Hockey game, I'm on my way home for dinner. Then the wife says your butt call is over. My husband is on his way home.

The Predators of Nashville are winning next year. Get ready for a fight, fight and fights to WIN, WIN, WIN. We want THE STANLY CUP THIS TIME.

Horse Racing

What is Horse Racing?

When people come together with the finest horses about the same age, to race them on a track with thousands of people betting money on a horse to win more money. It's all for the lucky ones.

They're off! You never know who is going to win. You beat the odds. The winner is fifteen, the worst horse in the race. No bet on him.

Some people spend their life savings on one race on one horse to win or lose. If I am betting I'm betting to win. I can't win if I lose.

People come from all over the world for the KENTUCKY DERBY. The horses have been training, taken care of for one race, and that what it's all about. Only one can win. I rather play for the one to win; losers don't get paid – problem solved.

Horses are great, all colors black, brown, tan, white. I don't care about the color; I just want one that will WIN.

Some people live to gamble on horses. Some people are like this. Will I buy dinner or play the horses? If it wins it's steak and lobster; the race is over, it's soup.

Some people have families and play the horses. Never take away your family. He's driving to the race; the races are over, but he's walking home.

I think horses talk to each other. (These are horses talking) You won last time. My little pony needs new shoes. Mine needs a new saddle. OK you can have this race, but I want the next one, OK.?

The KENTUCKY DERBY best horses in the world, all the money in the world. One horse wins, so why not bet on all the horses.? That way you can't lose. The race is over; it was a tie. NO one wins.

The best way to pick a winning horse is the strongest. NO the best way to pick a winning horse, the light in the weight. The best to pick a winning horse is to pick one that always wins – problem solved.

Has there ever been a horse that won every race it was in? YES, we have not found it yet.

Will the race today show us the best horse in the world? YES, if it ever shows up.

Are all horses rated to win? YES, although most of them will be losers; only one will win. Can't you bet for one to lose? NO, then they want a winner.

After the races are over, what goes on then? The winners get a lot of Butt Calls.

What is the best way to train a horse? Give him good food with great vitamins; run on a track longer than the one he's going to races on; the day of race tell him if you win you can have sex with that female horse over there. A Horse butt call – problem solved.

Do people ever get to meet the horse that they're going to bet on? Just before the race, the horses walk down and around the race track. The horse can give you a what's up; the horses talk to each other; they do know who is going to win.

Can the horses really talk? YES, horses talk with their horses talk like people talk with people. People talk is American talk. With horses, they are the same as Mexicans talk Mexican, Italians talk Italian, losers talk losers talk, winners talk winners talk – problem solved.

Hope you enjoyed the book
Ha Ha, the book of humor.

Bless You always. Keep laughing.

May God bless you today
and every day. Amen.

Century Gothic and AR HERMANN on 50# LSI crème white
Type and design by Karen Paul Stone